Rüc

The Oppression of Women

Genocide   Fear
Cover-up   Anger

Reprint or duplication only permitted with approval of the author. Use and distribution by non-authorized third parties in all printed, audiovisual, and acoustic media is prohibited. Copyright remains with the author. We are not liable for printing and sentence errors.

Legal information:
Dr. Rüdiger Opelt, Georg-Rendl-Weg 46, 5111 Bürmoos, Austria,
    Saw Partner
    r@opelt.com,   www.opelt.com

All rights reserved

KDP-ISBN: 9781694115218

Composition: Michael Opelt /Schörfling/**Saw** partner
Translation: Ian Steiner/Lambach, Austria/Seattle, WA,USA
                     steiner.ip@gmail.com
Copy-editing: Max Steiner/Seattle, WA, USA
Cover: Monika Steiner/Lambach

Origin German Edition "Die Unterdrückung der Frauen", Feb. 2019, KDP-ISBN: 9781796713831, by S.A.W. Edition, Salzburg, distributed also by amazon and kdp

        Book by S.A.W. Edition; **sawedition@gmail.com**

        Distribution by amazon

Salzburg 2019

Dedicated to our mother
another victim of war
widow and mother of sons
fair teacher of many children
She trusted the fathers and loved them
with all their faults
taught their narrative of history
looking for answers
for ninety years
Perhaps from heaven you will see
the dawn of a new time

I cite the works of other authors by listing the author's name and the year of publication in parentheses. The particular title of the book can be found in the bibliography. I recommend the listed books as further or concurrent reading, shedding further light on cited theories and any out of context quotes.

Contents

I. **Prehistory**   7
   A search for truth 7
   German violent trauma 8
   Suppressed genocide as cause for family conflict 12

II. **Matriarchy and Patriarchy**   19
   Behavior biological roots of violence 19
   In the Shadow of War 23
   Egalitarian matrifocal primal community..............................25
   Matrifocal advanced cultures..29
   The fairytale of the superior patriarchy 34
   War is the beginning of the end 36
   Senseless tyranny..38

III. **Genocides by the patriarchy**   40
   The Indo-Europeans 40
   Asia 41
   Africa 43
   Oppression and eradication 45
   War in the Middle Ages...47
   Genocide in the Muslim world 48
   The destruction of America...50
   The only good Indian is a dead Indian 51
   Colonialism, Imperialism, and Neocolonialism 53
   Modern nomadic invasions 56

IV. **The oppression of women**   60
   Worldwide genocide of women 60
   Origin of the "bad mother" 62
   Postpartum depression 65
   Infertility as an unconscious protest 67
   War of the Roses 69
   Abducted children...71
   Overweight epidemic 73

V. **The cover-up of violence**   76
   Genes contradict propaganda 76
   Attempts at matrifocal restauration 78
   Spiritual securing of power 82
   The Catholic church as an instrument of power and the ideological embellishment of oppression 85

Why Christmas does not bring peace 86
Invention of Fake-News 88
Secret Mithraism..90
And pigs can fly! 91
Schizophrenia as (schizophrenic due to) chronic denial of reality ...93
Patriarchal counter-reformation in church, politics, and science 96
Scientific dogma as a patriarchal instrument of power 98
Prejudices of historical science 101

VI. Healing of fear and anger   **105**
Fear and duress/compulsion..105
Causes of psychological illness..107
Patriarchosis..109
Awareness of war victims' suffering 111
Anger and aggression..112
Healing the violence epidemic 114
Jewish genocide coping strategy..114
Democracy 116
Truth and Reconciliation Commissions 119
Collective trauma therapy..121
Social learning 122

VII. Social balance   **125**
A lot will change 125
The upcoming paradigm shift 127
The answer lies in the ocean...128
World history retold..130
Gender-feminism as equalization on a patriarchal base.................133
Megatrend women 135
Egalitarian matrivivial future..137
The sanctity of birth 139
Investments in commitment and relationship.................................140
There is enough for everyone: equilibrium economy 141
Our true needs 146
A new global currency...148
A global movement to rescue Mother Earth....................................150

Acknowledgments   153
Bibliography   154
Readers' comments   157

A search for truth

What fuels the cruelty of humankind, which has oppressed and exploited enemies and fellow countrymen alike since the beginning of recorded history?

Why are the oppressed victims, without power and rights, most notably women?

Have the countless historically warranted violent acts left us as unimpaired as patriarchs and militants want us to believe, or are they rather the source of increasing mental issues?

These questions have concerned me throughout my entire professional life as a psychologist and psychotherapist.

40 years ago, while working as a young psychologist in child psychiatry, I was puzzled by the misery of many children and their families, even though they often did not have a lack of material goods. Those disastrous conditions haven't changed. Not until 2018 did Austrian health insurance companies acknowledge a deficiency of psychotherapeutic care for children, and have since promised improvement. Let us hope that going forward, our children will not be left alone with their anxieties and difficulties.

25 years ago I discovered that mental disorders can be traced back to the second world war and other traumas originating in violence. Experts tried to silence me by branding it "unscientific nonsense". This attitude changed in 2002, and many have since taken up the cause. My book "Die Kinder des Tantalus" has helped many to understand their personal history.

I have since discovered similar violent traumas worldwide and in all eras of time. This discovery may sound incredible given the historical misrepresentation perpetuated by historiography and the sciences, a practice which has been perfected and enforced by the Catholic church since the Constantinian shift (313 AD). Anyone not believing in the holy mass murderers (Constantine the Great,

Charlemagne, Otto the Great) was branded a heretic, tortured, and killed. It will arguably take years to be able to talk in this manner, without being silenced in one way or another.

The widespread preoccupation with national socialism nowadays is a good thing. Still, it is not a singular operational accident caused by a lunatic, as portrayed by the mainstream. Genocide has been the foundation of power for the patriarchal warrior caste since the Indo-Europeans first developed superior military technology by domesticating the horse 6000 years ago.

Past genocides perpetrated by the militant patriarchy follow us like a perpetual boomerang.

The extenuation of violence of the powerful leads to confusion, suffering, anguish, and anger.

Inclusion of women and their wisdom of life is the essential step towards a happier world.

German violent trauma

Why was it Germans, of all people, who perpetrated the Holocaust?

Why did Protestantism originate in Saxony?

Why was Communism founded in Germany?

Why did Leipzig citizens single-handedly overthrow the GDR?

Why is the Pegida so powerful in Saxony?

Numerous books have been written concerning all these questions, none of which give satisfying answers. It is an impossible task as long as the culture in question denies and suppresses its history of violence while embellishing and portraying it as sacred national acts.

World history has sadly been marked by genocide and its reinterpretation as sacred heroism since the emergence of the militant patriarchy, and German history is no exception. When Hitler lost the war, this pattern was broken and the Holocaust viewed with contempt. Acts of rehabilitation such as stumbling blocks, memorials, and rituals of reconciliation (Brandt's genuflection in Warsaw) have led Germany on to an internationally recognized, healthy path for the first time in its history,

Where does the incredible cruelty of the Nazis originate?

Psychology teaches us that, without reflection, victims of violence are likely to turn to violence themselves. (Opelt 2002) The Holocaust as we know it is backed by 2000 years of genocides, which have been idealized and camouflaged with "sacred" notions, similar to Soviet propaganda rebranding Stalin, a mass murderer, as "Father Stalin" and "Savior of the Fatherland". (Opelt 2016)

In the 20th century, mass media helped uncover most genocides (Hitler, Stalin, Mao, Khmer Rouge, Rwanda, Srebrenica, Armenia, Boers) and, for the first time in history, were not viewed as heroic deeds. This is a new development. In all wars prior to World War I, the victors would idealize their genocide, turning it into righteous heroism.

Therefore, to process our disposition to violence and anger, we must look further than the Holocaust, and acknowledge all hushed up genocides in Central Europe.

I want to illustrate this by looking at the Saxons and Sorbs:

The territory covering present-day Lower Saxony was the preferred battleground of the Romans starting in 14 AD, in retaliation for the defeat they suffered to the Saxon tribes at the Teutoburg Forest. Emperors would have to prove their competence by leading a campaign against the Germanic peoples, resulting in Saxons and their fellow peoples suffering genocide almost every generation. (Moosbauer 2018) First there was Roman general Germanicus, who eradicated the entire Marsi population. The killing did not stop until after Charlemagne's thirty year war against the Saxons, who he had killed in substantial numbers, even after they had surrendered.

100 years later, Saxon dukes processed their trauma by traditional means: In the capacity of German kings, they attacked the Slavic population between Elbe and Oder and inflicted the same pain that they had experienced themselves. The territory that was to become the GDR was oppressed and exploited for 200 years. The Slavs indeed defended themselves, although revolts were only successful in the North for a while. Sorbs living in the area of the present-day Free State of Saxony were exploited by an existing Germanic upper-class for 600 years starting in 930 AD: They were forced to compulsory labor under the Germans (Six weekdays work for their earls, sunrise to sundown), as well as being taxed for any work done in the little free time they had. Enforced Christianization also meant paying a tithe to the bishopric. These conditions were getting close to killing through labor, with which Hitler wanted to exterminate all non-Aryans. In the same way, the Spaniards eradicated the Caribbean Indians in a matter of a few decades. Daily rape (Jus primae noctis) and resulting German-Sorb mixed offspring broke the Sorbs.

Resettlers from present-day Franconia arrived in depopulated areas, freed of compulsory labor and taxes, which were assigned to surviving Sorbs. Their impotent rage, accumulated over centuries, has been left unresolved until today. and inhabits the mixed descendants without them knowing the origin of their anger.

In 1517, this rage manifested itself as the protestant revolution of Martin Luther, who worked in Saxon territory (Wittenberg, Wartburg), where he established the first protestant townships. The Duke of Saxony saved Luther's life and stopped Saxon protestants from being killed or imprisoned (Jan Hus of the Czech Republic was still burned at the stake). The Catholic church provoked Luther's and the farmers' revolt by constantly imposing new taxes and exploiting Germany as a whole.

The Catholic church had become a mundane repression society in the Middle Ages, and was not going to admit defeat. The main setting for the religious wars, their climax being 1618 - 1648, was the assimilated area of the Polabian Slavs, and it lost 50% of its population (2nd genocide).

The German revolution in 1848 spawned the egalitarian communistic idea of Marx and Engels, but the social insurgencies turned bloody and all seditionists executed.

After 1945 Eastern Germany (including displaced people) had to especially pay for crimes perpetrated by the Nazis, by enduring another 45 years of dictatorship. Communism was embraced as a return to egalitarian Slavic society, but soon debunked as a secret police (Stasi) sham.

In 1989, Leipzig citizens felled the GDR single-handedly, cast out their oppressors (peaceful revolution), and were a significant factor in ending the Soviet dictatorship.

The Western colonization had been suppressed for 1000 years, and subsequently repeated itself in a pattern similar to 930: the erstwhile GDR depopulated and destabilized itself dramatically over a few decades. These disappointments congregate in the Pegida movement.

Processes like these are the same worldwide and are similar to the violence against Jews (for 2600 years) and the Irish (for 1000 years). Both peoples had established a written tradition before the genocide started, recorded and recalled violence, and know until today why and against what they are defending themselves. The awareness of the North Ireland conflict as well as the Palestine conflict are therefore being made accessible and has, in the case of Ireland, already lead to an act of reconciliation (elimination of border barriers).

Most peoples on this Earth are not aware of genocides they suffer or perpetrate, therefore the atrocities continue repeatedly, and the rage of the victims is endless. The Catholic church was a substantial part of the oppression machinery, pursuing both physical and cultural extinction (whosoever refused brainwash, called compulsory Christianization, was burned at the stake).

The anger of victims and their descendants will only end if the violence is called out by its name and resolved through acts of reconciliation. It needs perpetrator-victim-rituals at family constellations seminars and political gestures of reconciliation on a national level, which will only work when respect is shown for the victims.

Suppressed genocide as cause for family conflict

My experiences as a psychologist have taught me that a majority of mental disorders can be traced back to violent trauma in various forms. Maniacs are not insane, but rather the relation of cause and effect is displaced and suppressed to a point, at which not even psychiatrists can identify the causes.

I suffered from depression as a young man. My father took me to see a psychiatrist, who explained that my problems were endogenic, meaning my brain was sick, and that I would have to swallow pills for the rest of my life. This did not make sense to me, so I tossed out the pills (which did not help me anyway), and studied clinical psychology to find the right answers.

Over the course of many self-awareness sessions, I started to understand the causes of my fears and gained confidence. I sought out depth psychologists, who traced my fears back to experiences of my childhood, and I got better as we worked through them. At the end of my time at university I felt equipped to help others through the same process of healing.

This process proved difficult in child psychiatry. Depth psychology was too involved and costly for low income clients. Furthermore, systemic short-term therapy and depth psychology were only useful up to a certain point, and sick children kept suffering from relapses

Epidemiological evaluation of hundreds of cases showed correlation of trauma and symptoms, in that the traumatic cause and exhibited form of the symptom often match. Aggressive violence causes aggressive disorders, oppression causes fear, sexual and physical abuse cause physical symptoms such as anorexia and eating disorders.

The complication was grandchildren developing symptoms related to trauma experienced by their grandparents. This was (and still is) interpreted as a genetically induced disease, which was treated with medication.

By now psychotherapy has established a systemic approach which can adequately explain the correlations present in a grandparents-parents-children system.

I experimented with ways of explaining the discovered traumas, meaning the truth, to patients and their families. It proved successful and unlocked the strength for self-healing. My patients were no longer categorized as lunatic, but rather began to understand their feelings of anger and fear. They no longer felt pitied as mentally ill patients, and transformed into experts on one's own account.

The human brain functions as a super computer. A computer crashing without known reason can cause anger or panic. An expert explaining the reasons for the system outage and what component has to be updated leads to reassurance and the right steps to fix the computer.

Psychology, as do engineering and pathophysiological medicine, deals with finding and correcting errors. Medicine's fruitless search of mainly the biological hardware of the brain, which has not yet been adequately explored, results in many psychiatric patients staying chronically ill.

Experience, memories, realizations, and feelings are human software, which has been explored for 150 years. Psychotherapy presents various options to reprogram one's brain by changing behaviour.

This process is done quickly if the crucial software error is found. We now know that subsequently the hardware will repair itself, given the brain's plasticity.

In the 1980s I was working with children whose grandparents had suffered traumas during World War II. These families were living under victim-perpetrator conditions, either scared of persecution and enemies or otherwise unable to reflect on their aggressive behavior. Once parents/children were able to identify perpetrators and victims within their family history, their own behavior became comprehensible and symptoms disappeared. In the process, perpetrator-families proved to be as traumatized as victim-families, however the suppression of perpetrator-guilt was perpetuated longer than the victims' barrier against pain, therefore it took longer for perpetrator-families to seek therapy. They have since started to face their past, and are able to rid themselves of anorexia, paranoia, and depression.

Family lines which include both perpetrators and victims are impacted the most. Symptom carriers experienced an inner battle of their past, and exhibited especially difficult and chronic psychosomatic disorders. Tough situations like these were cured by family constellation therapy.

In the process of working through experiences of the whole family, my patients got better and better. I was feeling great myself in the meantime. My fears had disappeared and had been replaced with the wonderful feeling of competence.

A fragment remained, despite 40 years of self-awareness and supervision. Injustices still made me angry, sometimes fuming with rage to a point of losing composure. What caused this anger?

While we had dealt with and pacified World War II, I was not the only family member with anger issues. Disputes kept arising and even when a factual, objective resolution had already been accepted, emotions were still running high. Inheritance disputes required a lot of energy, although we usually reached a fair solution for all. Situations as this are not unique to our family, but I felt irritated that my psychological instruments were not enough to establish peace among my family.

Did I have to expand my system and uncover an even deeper layer yet?

I have reflected extensively on conflicts within my family and families of clients over the past 15 years. I call my family's psychological pattern the "Slight of the Cheated". We share this pattern with thousands of other families, calling it "the quarrel of father and uncle". Our uncle disowned and took advantage of our father because he lived abroad at the time our grandfather died. This slight tormented our father until his death.

Even our grandfather was taken advantage of. He was ousted by a Saxon lignite mining company which proceeded to tear down his hometown and dig a huge pit. Though our grandfather was remunerated for his house, this happened during the 1923 hyperinflation, and the money was worthless in a matter of days. Grandmother and grandfather argued and suffered because of this until the end of their days.

My brothers and I are aware of these facts, nonetheless we seem to carry affront and anger toward these injustices within us. Many discussions led to each one of us to feel like the victim, being taken advantage of by the others.

Was there more history to this persistent pattern?

I looked further. Our great grandfather was a farmer in Saxony, whose fields were also swallowed by a ligate pit; fields which had been in our family for generations. How then had the Opelts come into possession of these fields?

This question led me on a journey into the history of the Free State of Saxony. The thing about owning fields there over the last 1000 years is that back then, present day Saxons were Sorbs. For 300 years, proper Saxons from Lower Saxony, Saxony-Anhalt, and

Westphalia harassed the Sorbs with war and oppression, took their land and exploited them (see last chapter). The Holy Slavic Crusade of Henry the Lion ultimately led to Slavic lands becoming the first German colony, eventually being renamed as "Saxony". A small "Indian reservation" persevered at the Elbe, and inhabitants still speak Sorian today.

The same thing happened concurrently in Ireland: Normans and Anglo-Saxons massacred the Irish, took their fields, and had them cultivate their expropriated fields as slaves of English lords. The anger exhibited by the IRA traces back to this 1000 year long oppression of England's oldest colony. A few Gaelic territories survived in the West, more "Indian reservations".

The fact that there now is free Ireland means the consequences of these violent acts have been documented. In Sorbic territory the oppression was overarching, including eliminating its name, renaming it Saxony, and suppressing and forgetting its history. Saxon's have forgotten the reason they fight, even though Leipzig citizens ("We are the people") nearly single-handedly toppled the GDR, and Saxony native group Pegida acts almost as fanatical as the IRA.

What did everyday life look like for a Sorb (Irish) in the 12th century?

Fields were stolen by occupying forces, nonetheless one had to cultivate them as bond-slave, in service of the thieves. There were no rights, money, or dignity. Women were raped by occupiers, some only had a chance of survival as concubines. Many Sorb-Saxon children were born. Are they not bound to have accumulated a destructive, impotent rage over the centuries?

What are the consequences?

Nearly all Saxons are descendants of both Germanic oppressors and

Slavic victims. Our ancestors suffered the same injustice as all colonized peoples of the last 500 years. Except they suffered twice as long. Church and emperor persuaded them that it was for their best and a noble part of the progress of civilization.

Having both perpetrators and victims as ancestors is the most difficult condition of family constellations. One grandfather is a perpetrator (Nazi, occupier, earl, etc.), the other a victim (Jew, Indio, day laborer, etc.), thus the family includes perpetrator and victim, which frequently makes one ill. If this condition is denied, the perpetrator-victim-game repeats itself in each new generation.

Someone is the perpetrator, seizing hold of anything they can.

The other is the victim, getting taken advantage of.

It is easy to argue among brothers in this manner, even if nobody knows why.

Numbers and facts are of no importance for these arguments. It is the emotions of people who are cast into adversarial roles, which have to be reconciled by releasing the other of their antagonistic role.

My anger has calmed since discovering these correlations. However I was alone with my realization because neither psychologists nor family constellations therapists were able to conceive how something could continue to have an effect 1000 years later.

I realized that I had to develop a new method which incorporated not only contemporary history, but the comprehensive history of a region as well.

This method needs two things:

The first part of the book shows the evolution of violence throughout history and its impact on peoples and families. Patriarchal structures play a major role, as does the global uprising of oppressed women we face today.

The second part describes how patients and families can free themselves of violent structures. If done in large numbers, this will lead to a more peaceful world, one that does no longer harm humans and nature.

II. Matriarchy and Patriarchy

Behavior biological roots of violence

There are two diametrically opposed theories concerning the origin of humankind's exceptional readiness to use violence.

    1. theory of university sciences

    2. criticism of patriarchy

1. Let us begin with official theses found in science books, written by university professors:

Aggression is part of life and important for survival. (Lorenz 1998) Animals kill or are killed, and defend themselves so as to not be eaten.

Predators are of importance in any ecosystem, where they induce evolution of prey and get rid of sick and weak specimen. Genetic mistakes are quickly sorted out. Predators and prey are racing each other. Ungulates get faster and nimbler, and predators have to keep devising new strategies in order to feed.

Predators do not kill in cruelty. Biting the throat kills quickly, and the prey feels little pain during the following adrenaline rush. Before it knows what's happening, it is done. A short, quick death without prolonged suffering, only granted to humans as a heart attack.

Predators are presently the topic of much discussion due to the return of the wolf to Central Europe. Some want to get rid of the wolves straightaway, whereas biologists remind us that an ecosystem with wolves is significantly healthier than without. (Which practically means that wolves are better at regulating species diversity than human hunters)

Animals prefer living without natural enemies. Our jungle ancestors were safe on top of trees. Chimpanzees are only violent towards their own kind when they go to war against another group of chimpanzees. Famed primate researcher Jane Goodall was shocked when she discovered how cruel her dear subjects could be. Thankfully, warmongering behavior among Chimpanzees is rare. So far there is no consensus whether it is due to protein deficiency, or extreme territorial density caused by deforestation of the rainforest.

There are limits to the aggression of predators. They fight to feed and reproduce. Prey can approach a well-fed predator in peace, and he will allow it until he is hungry again.

After the East African jungles disappeared 5 million years ago, our australopithecine ancestors relocated to the Savanna, suddenly finding themselves in the category of prey. Slower prey than gazelles too, as such very welcomed by lions and leopards. Though they sometimes managed to save themselves by climbing a tree, they remained prey to predators for the next three million years. The propagation of humanoids had some major starting troubles.

How to deal without quick feet or hooves?

Think, think, think! Humans do it still when encountering a difficult situation, and in the process slowly developed larger brains.

They discovered that survival was easier in larger groups. 20 or 30 monkeys had a bigger chance at fending off a herd of lions. Waving arms and shrill yelling was often enough, and the level of communication needed to coordinate further encouraged brain growth.

Even more effective was pelting lions with stones, and warding them off with sticks. Sticks and stones were arguably the first weapons of defense.

Homo habilis made the discovery of sharpening stones and sticks around 2.5 million years ago, which created a sort of draw situation with lions. Habilis humans even dared to approach a lion's kill and eat leftovers, especially bone marrow which they exposed with sharp rocks.

At some point either Homo rudolfensis, Homo ergaster, or Homo erectus discovered the act of throwing a stick with the possibility of killing a lion. Humankind's first weapon, the javelin, was born. Homo erectus' muscles and body structure evolved into a refined javelin sling. Predator human was born.

This new predator quickly spread across Africa and Eurasia. New finds in China, dating 2.1 million years, suggest that even ancestors of homo erectus had ventured there.

The combination of large brains, group hunting, and spear weapons enabled humans to hunt and exterminate all large land animals, as well as whales. 5000 years after arriving in North America, humans had hunted all large animals to extinction.

This was a real shock for hunters spoilt by success. They realized that Mother Nature had to be treated with care. It was the origin of the ecological religion of Indian natives, and a peaceful matrifocal primal civilization in Europe.

Early agricultural farmers were also devoted to peaceful dealings with the environment, calling it Mother Earth. Women had command of the fields which were fruitful only when one was on good terms with Mother Nature.

The development of livestock farming reintroduced animals for consumption. This led to competition for grazing land to ensure a steady growth of livestock.

Predators kill the young of their rivals, which acts as natural birth control because their numbers are dependent on available prey. Too many predators will cause prey to go extinct, as humans had already experienced themselves.

Humans had learned to form ever-growing groups in order to

conquer larger territories for livestock breeding. Agricultural farmers were additional prey to be assaulted, and their supplies stolen. Furthermore, if their wives were taken and their warriors assimilated into one's own army, even larger territories, livestock, and agricultural land could be established or captured.

It was the birth of the patriarchy, its essential motives being war and conquest for the accumulation of resources. The patriarchy, as its name infers, is a creation of men, whereas women chose a very different path.

2. History of humanity viewed through criticism of the patriarchy:

Doris Wolf (2017) presents prehistory from a perspective most people have yet to experience. She sees prehistoric artifacts not as remnants of mammoth and buffalo hunters, but as witnesses to a peaceful culture living of vegetables and fish, a diet which doctors recommend as healthy today. Wolf upends our world image, flips arrowheads and axe heads upside down, and describes them as ritual amulets, shaped like the vulva, embodying the great Goddess. She similarly identifies the vulva within circles and triangles. The great pyramids of Egypt symbolize the three forms of the Goddess and were built at the crest of the Nile delta, in itself the form of the vulva, long before the patriarchy existed.

Is she allowed to make this claim, to argue for an alternative to the great historic hunters, an image implanted in us for 200 years?

She is. It is perfectly legitimate to interpret history from the perspective of a woman. Any historians protesting this are well reminded that they have been perpetuating an explicitly male theory for 200 years. (It was exclusively men projecting their views onto the past) The mere existence of an alternative theory shows that neither one is proven to be true. We just don't know, therefore it is time to scientifically examine both alternatives. True science needs two alternative hypotheses to be examined, in order for one to emerge as the more plausible one. Prehistory has so far evaded empiricism by banning the female theory from universities.

To think, verification would be so simple. If blood on the "arrowheads" is found to be human (menstrual blood), they are ritual vulvas, and if it is mammoth or animal blood, they are hunting weapons. All one has to do is test it instead of looking down on theories presented by "feminists". In the same vein one could dismiss hunting theories presented by "virilists".

For Doris Wolf and her comrades the patriarchy was established by the Indo-Europeans 6000 years ago, its essential motives being war and conquest for the accumulation of resources. The patriarchy, as its name infers, is a creation of men, whereas women chose a very different path.

You, dear reader, have to decide which version you think more plausible and desirable. Despite all "facts", neither thesis has been empirically examined, thus we do not know the answer. You may postpone your decision until you have finished the book and know all facts. Let me tell you the details of the male and female perspective.

In the Shadow of War

Genus homo sapiens was crowned ruling species on Earth through its bellicose contact with its human, animal, and plant environment. (it is merely unclear whether this happened 2 million or 6000 years ago) Human body mass and that of their domesticated animals makes up 97% of the world's vertebrate biomass. (30% humans, 67% dom. animals, 3% wild animals)

Such dominance of a single species has existed once before: A carbon enriched environment enabled trees to grow rampant, their waste polluting rivers and seas, until nature collapsed (Remnants of the catastrophe are found in coal seams). The following extinction of species reduced trees to a healthy balance, becoming the embodiment of peaceful nature.

Evolution allows for extreme developments and corrects them once the ecological foundation is endangered. Many animals exhibit so-called extreme organs which first allow them to prosper before killing them off. The giant deer (Irish elk) used its enormous antlers to triumph over competitors, only to starve when it got stuck between trees.

Mankind's extreme organs are its brain, social skills, and weapon technology. Our cognitive skills conquered the world, our social skills led to ever growing tribal organization, and our weapons vanquished any foe. Our efficiency is such that soon all of our food sources will be destroyed. In the far future, aliens may find remnants of mankind in an archaeological trash layer, which they will mine for plastic and metal to rebuild civilization on Earth.

And yet, our extreme organ brain gives us flexibility. Whenever our food source has been depleted, we simply looked for a different one. After the extinction of large game we developed agriculture. After eating all land animals, we turned to whales and fish. When hunting no longer put food on the table, we started breeding live stock. After ridding the ocean of its fish, we built aqua farms. Experts presently recommend eating insects, which would last us at least 100 years.

Our brains even let us control our evolution by enabling us to identify when we have reached deep waters and a dwindling source of survival. That point in time is now!

When the giant deer recognized the danger of his large antlers, it was already too late. It could not shed its antlers, and died off.

We can see the drawbacks of the human selfish brain and patriarchal weapon technology. The drop of the first atom bomb crossed the line, things had to change, and wars have drastically decreased in numbers since Hiroshima and Nagasaki in 1945.

We have reached the point of knowing that wars are not necessarily the final solution of a problem, but it has been the rule of the stronger patriarch for 6000 years, and still is.

In order to survive we need to revert to our human roots and a community that has existed since the birth of Homo sapiens until 4000 BC (98% of our species' existence):

Egalitarian matrifocal primal community

I must thank Kirsten Armbruster, who, in her book "Das Muttertabu" (2010), provided the final piece to my theoretical framework to heal our civilization. During my student years I was spurned on by the lectures of Ernest Bornemann, an ethnologist, who had researched North American matrilineal cultures and postulated a cooperative prehistory, which was then destroyed by the patriarchy. (Ancient Greeks among others) Ever since I have been looking for traces of a time less bellicose than the last 6000 years. Within the Tantalus myth I discovered the metaphor for patriarchal violence, ever responsible for spiritual malady. (Opelt 2002, 2009, 2016) Books written by male historians and psychiatrists aroused my suspicion that the most important insights into the course of history and suffering of the psyche were covered up or overlooked. I was alone with my belief, and my theses were brushed off as "non-science" by university researchers.

Kirsten Armbruster makes it very clear: Humans spent 98% of their developmental period living as a matrivivial-avuncular tribal community. Women were the core of the community, for they bore children. The importance of the sperm was seen as insignificant or overlooked. The mother's brothers would help to protect and feed her children. Sexuality was openly displayed and showed a joyful embrace of life, while chemotaxis inhibited incest. Paternity was neither verifiable nor important. It was not until the South Russian Indo-Europeans discovered the possibility of a single bull impregnating multiple cows that they started breeding with a purpose. After domesticating the horse and inventing the chariot, they used their superior weapons to spread the patriarchy, culminating in the Inquisition, burning of witches, and colonizing of the entire world. The Inquisition was the climax of disempowerment of the feminine. For 6000 years patriarchs led the world into war and began destroying Mother Earth. This incremental triumphant advance of the patriarchy is reflected in the development of religious concepts: The birthing primal mother changed to the Sacred Wedding, to the secondary wife of a male God, ending with a strictly male, monotheistic God. This spiritual degradation of women went along with the disenfranchisement of all subjects by male rulers.

Armbruster uses impressive ethnological and historical documents as a foundation for her thesis of a patriarchal cultural fracture. Depictions and statues of fertile and birthing women are found all throughout the paleolithic and mesolithic periods. Sacred mountains, cave and spring sanctuaries, as well as the syllables Ma and Ana have endured as witnesses to the Great Mother Goddess in all languages and cultures.

Reading Armbruster's books helped me see clearly: "The Lord is my shepherd"; Abel is the "good shepherd", who tends to his sheep in order to kill and eat them. Cain is condemned as an agricultural farmer. Feminine sexuality is the work of the devil. The Bible religions are a product of a patriarchal herdsman culture. The Tantalus myth, primal myth of patriarchal violence, reflects the disempowerment of the ancient maternal religion: The Goddess' power is to give life, thus the Father God can only take life. Tantalus kills his son to impress his father Zeus. Child murder was deemed sacrilegious by the Greeks, leading to spiritual sickness and suffering within the family for the next five generations. Even so, sacrilegious murder was perpetuated and worshiped throughout frequent wars. Roman patriarchs even had the right to kill their own children, which indeed they did. Every dictator throughout history built their empires on the killing of rivals and their children. More patriarchal power led to a wider expansion of the killings, from children to whole tribes of peoples. Genocide and the fear of it became important pillars of power and were thus turned into epics by patriarchal religions.

Even though matrivivial knowledge has been blanketed by catholic legends, it still exists: 60 years ago I was squeezing through the Blasenstein in St. Thomas (Upper Austria). I thought this to be a thrilling experience, but the claim that this rock was miraculous because a pastor was mummified by it sounded rather strange. Thanks to Armbruster (2018) I now know that these rocks with crawl spaces are found throughout Europe, and passing through one is performing a healing ritual of sacred birth. Furthermore, nouns like Kall, Hall, Hel, Holle, or Quelle share a paleolithic stem meaning "cave sanctuary", providing a new perspective of the cities Hallein and Hallstadt, beyond their association with salt. (The Celts called salt Hall because it came from a cave [Hall]). Armbruster talks about the Camino de Santiago and the Basques' pilgrimage to the End of the World for 10,000 years. There, Mother Water leads souls into Heaven before they are reborn in Mother's lap. Women used to rub against cup-marked stones, for souls would gather in springs and basins and slip into the woman's belly. I learned that the seashell is the feminine symbol of the Goddess, which the Christians could not eliminate and therefore re-branded as the symbol of Santiago the Slayer of Moors.

I searched for definite explanations of history for 50 years, with few reasonable results (historic sciences claim that nothing is provable and personal interpretation is unacceptable, resulting in a monopoly of opinion based on patriarchal interpretations by academic professors). I have logically concluded that the Basques are Europe's native population, and Armbruster verifies it. She also explains the particulars of a 1000 year long falsification of culture by the catholic manifestation of the patriarchy: pilgrimages to black Madonnas are matriarchal pilgrim rituals, which have been changed to the Christian Virgin Mary. The accompanying Christian legends are outrageous: Mother Mary was not black, holy Mother Earth was indeed.

Archaeology and historic sciences perpetuate the falsification of history to a point of reinterpreting paleolithic female statuettes as penis-vulva-symbols. The female bosom became the male testicles, the woman's head was now the penis, and the male genitalia was naturally placed above the female. How far can this bastardization go?

Armbruster's books explained a lot of my past experiences. As an adolescent I drew a picture of a cave entrance in the shape of a vulva, from which sprang a red stream, and above there flew a crow. Reading Armbruster (2014) I realized that I had drawn a cave sanctuary with ritualistic menstrual blood and crow as a symbol of metamorphosis. It also addressed a discontent I had felt in my religious studies class. The theological nonsense becomes intelligible, if it is understood as a disavowal of the great Mother Goddess. The Virgin Mary is the live-giving Goddess. Caspar, Melchior, and Balthazar are the three forms of Goddess, worshiped in the twelve days after Christmas. The Holy Trinity of Life (Becoming, Growing, Metamorphosis) is reinterpreted as masculine Father, Son, and Holy Ghost. One does not have to believe every claim Armbruster makes, even so, her theory of a motherly world makes more sense than all religions glorifying violence and suffering, or excusing it as God given. Why have faith in a religion which charges into "holy" wars with blessed weapons, a religion with a God who demanded the death of his son, the ritualistic consumption of Christ's flesh, and the killing of people of different faith?

Armbruster's observations are based on the discoveries of archaeologist Marija Gimbutas (2010): In neolithic Southeastern Europe there existed a cult of the great Goddess, who manifested as Water Goddess, snake symbols, labyrinths, Bird Goddess with bird heads, butterfly, double axe, queen bee, crescent moon, and bullhorns, depicted in thousands of artifacts. Many thousand clay, ivory, and stone figurines portray a complex symbolism, identifying itself through masks, dances, and spiritual rituals as a predecessor of Greek tragedy. Not until the arrival of Indo-Europeans did male Gods come into existence, slowly replacing the great Goddess in her functions. Minoan Crete with its snake priestesses, bull horns, and double axes was the highpoint of old European maternal religion. A continuous matrifocal development from the paleolithic to the Minoans exists. The old European culture was destroyed by the Indo-Europeans, though many old European symbolics survived as part of Greek culture. Thus Father God is only a few thousand years old, while Mother Goddess has been with us since the beginning.

Scientific consensus recognizes Greek culture to have developed by adopting Minoan components. What happened before is subject of discussion. Harald Haarmann sheds light on the issue (Haarmann 2017): Agriculture was brought from the Middle East to Thessaly in 6000 BC, and was soon adopted by all Danube tribes. They combined the new technology with their religion of the great Mother, creating a peaceful civilization. They developed scripture and metalworking (copper, gold, silver) around 5000 BC, 2000 years before the Sumerians. Shipbuilding emerged along the Danube and its many tributaries, the rivers acting as trade routes between large trading posts. (Vinca near Belgrade had 8,000 inhabitants)

In Southern Ukraine the Danube culture encountered the Indo-European kurgan culture, which had domesticated the horse and harnessed it to a carriage. During three migration periods between 4400 and 3000 BC, Indo-Europeans forced out the Danube culture, leading to displaced survivors settling on Greek islands. On Crete they developed the Minoan culture, perpetuating matriarchal structures of Danube culture and refining their script to Linear A.

This course of history corresponds with A. Toynbee's theory (1970), stating that every advanced civilization at its peak is destroyed by barbaric invasion and replaced by a subsidiary civilization after some dark centuries. In this way the Danube culture became Minoan, which in turn evolved into Greek culture.

The fascinating point of this thesis is that the world's first civilization was doing fine without patriarchal hierarchy and power.

Matrifocal advanced cultures

History class taught us that civilization originated in Mesopotamia and Egypt, where mighty kings went to war to unite the lands, and kept peace with an efficient administrative hierarchy. Romans and Chinese emperors perpetuated this tradition, instilling in us a history of great men, powerful administrations, and wars as a necessary evil.

This picture of history may be due to the fact that historic research started with the examination of written records. Whatever documents scholars were able to read all concerned kings and their wars, a situation welcomed by the male rulers of the 18th and 19th century.

As a student at a humanistic secondary high school, I always wondered why the first thing we studied in Latin class was Caesar's Gallic war, as well as Homer's Trojan war in Greek class. These were supposed to be witness accounts of great ancient cultures? War, war, and more war? Today we know that Caesar's forays into Gaul were mass murder, killing one million and enslaving another million. "De Bello Gallico" is propaganda designed to prepare Caesar's takeover in Rome. The Gallic genocide may perhaps play a part in the Frenchman's readiness to protest, still being genetically Gaul.

The fact that ancient writings speak of victorious patriarchs means neither that history has always been that brutal, nor that civilization didn't exist before the year 3300 BC. On the contrary! Archaeologists have found many humanly artifacts dating from 50,000 to 3300 BC. They showed mainly women with pronounced fertility features: Vulva, breasts, belly, birthing position.

These findings did not coincide with the common idea of heroic hunters turned mighty kings. Instead of drawing the logical conclusion that women played a substantially more important role in the Stone Age than in Antiquity, Middle Ages, and modern times, scholars settled the question with a scientificity similar to a Denkverbot (ban on thinking): Nothing could be said for sure about the "Venus" statues because there was no written tradition.

This ban on interpretation serves to protect the unproven premise that civilization was developed by men, and historians are indeed allowed to fantasize in this avenue, and include myths of heroic mammoth hunters in our textbooks.

Then there was Marija Gimbutas, Harvard professor, and expert of prehistory. In 1956, she discovered that the world's first civilization arose 2000 years before the Sumerans, in the Danube territory. It was matrifocal and developed the first documented script. Naturally her findings were contested, since they did not match the common historic dogma. When Gimbutas started talking about a great Mother Goddess, she was not taken seriously, and her death in 1994 put an end to the problem.

Whosoever took up Gimbutas theory of a Mother Goddess had no chance of a scientific career and had to publish their books in the academic Out as Books on Demand. It was all women, infected by radical feminism, which had no business at universities.

Too bad that the Danube script has been comprehensively documented by linguist Haarmann (2010). Stranger still the fact that metalworking (copper, gold) was developed by the Danube culture, their mines and smithies proven to be older than any found in other areas. Likewise the Danube shipping routes established on the Danube and its tributaries, creating a first, large trading network for the benefit of all Balkans inhabitants.

Universal historian Arnold Toynbee states that every advanced culture attracts barbaric tribes looking for riches, the ensuing raids leading it to collapse. Toynbee proved this claim for all known civilizations 80 years ago. At that time, Danube culture had not been explored yet, or he would have most certainly identified the barbarians involved in the trajectory of the world's first advanced culture. In this case, it was the Indo-Europeans hailing from the South Russian steppes, whose kurgan culture bordered Danube culture in the Dnjepr region. Militarily superior, having domesticated the horse and developed the chariot, the Indo-Europeans overwhelmed the peaceful, matrifocal Danube civilization. Around 3000 BC, the world's first civilization was history.

According to Toynbee, from the ruins of any culture emerges a subsidiary culture, continuing the old traditions. Survivors of Danube culture fled to the Greek islands and formed Minoan civilization on Crete and Santorin. Protected by the sea and the largest fleet at the time, the Minoans did not think highly of war, and preferred to invest in trade with eastern Mediterranean countries.

The Greek Mycenes, for all their warmongering, stood no chance against the Minoans and adopted their culture. Ultimately, a volcanic eruption on Santorin as well as a tsunami crippled the Crete fleet to such a degree that Crete was conquered by the Greeks around 1450 BC, wiping out the matriarchy. Still, the Minoans of eastern Crete survived until the 12th century, and their wise women passed on their tradition in secret.

Similar things transpired in Egypt. The first pharaoh, Narmer's conquest of the Nile delta in 3000 BC marked not the beginning, but the end of the advancement of Egyptian civilization. Agriculture in the Nile delta arose around 6500 BC, during matrifocal times. Doris Wolf proved that the matrifocal culture in Egypt took 3000 years to develop. The first hieroglyphic script emerged 300 years before Narmer, who hailed from Abydos in Upper Egypt, a region which was civilized late by Lower Egypt. Again it was the patriarchal border community conquering the parent culture and turning it into a male governed kingdom. Many historians have questioned the conquest of northern Egypt by now, instead embracing the idea of a peaceful unification of Egypt, centuries before Narmer.

Sumeria, the "cradle of civilization", is a late development. Every important discovery attributed to the Sumerians was actually made during the long stretch of time from 10,000 BC (agriculture) until 3300 BC, prior to the Sumerians' journey south from the Caucasus to conquer the estuary area of Euphrates and Tigris. There had not yet been a patriarchal system in Sumeria, but a trade network of cities. Trade led to the riches of Uruk, supposedly the world's first city. (Vinca was 2000 years older) The only original feature of Uruk was the ziggurat, a man-made mountain of clay bricks. We know mountain sanctuaries to be symbols of matrifocal Goddess cults. Since there were no natural mountains in the Mesopotamian alluvial plains, an artificial one had to be built so that the God or Goddess could take their customary place on top of the mountain/ziggurat.

The first large, patriarchal empire existed 1000 years later, ruled by Sargon II of Akkad, a descendant of semitic nomads. Whether men were in charge during the Sumerian creative period from 3300 to

2200 BC, of that there is no evidence.

The best mathematicians and philosophers have always come from India. We use Indian numbers, although they are erroneously called Arabic, practice Yoga, and study Indian spirituality. The Indian holy books (Bagavadgita, Mahabharata) were written during the rule of Aryan kings, reinforcing the patriarchal world view of Europe's Indo-European tribes.

Indian culture originated significantly earlier from Dravidian, dark skinned peoples, nowadays found exclusively in southern India. The peak of Indus culture was 2800 to 1800 BC, when it encompassed Baluchistan, Afghanistan, Rajastan, the Western Ganges region, reaching to Gujarat, north of Mumbai. It was the world's largest civilization at the time. Dravidians invented city planning based on rectangular blocks, along with fired bricks, sewage system, aqueducts, and the bathhouse. No signs of lordship were found in the cities Mohenjo-Daro and Harappa: no palaces, no monumental temples. The largest structures turned out to be warehouses. The Indus culture was a matrifocal, mercantile culture, similar to the Danube culture. The first open sea harbor was located in Lothal, in Gujarat, its ships fit for traveling to southern Mesopotamia. Indo-Europeans conquered the Indus culture in 1500 BC. They established kingdoms and subjugated the natives by implementing the lingering caste system. Some matrifocal traditions were preserved; vegetarianism and sacredness of animals, which it is forbidden to kill.

The patriarchies of the Inca and Aztecs were likewise late developments. Aztecs were a matrilineal culture. Little is known about Chavin culture in Peru and the Olmecs at the gulf of Mexico. Neither was militant.

To summarize: Interpreting the patriarchy as a constant of world history is a fallacy, originating from the inability of European researchers to read and understand extinct, non-Indo-European languages. (Deciphering of Egyptian language was entirely based on the Rosetta stone already being translated into Greek) Indo-European researcher from across the globe compiled their world view from recorded Indo-European testimonies. Indo-Europeans, the devisers of the militant patriarchy, have been defending patriarchal structures until today.

Early civilizations did indeed emerge from matrifocal or egalitarian cultures, their achievements plundered by barbaric hordes. European culture and all its knowledge traces back to matrifocal Danube culture and Minoan Crete culture. The great Indian culture was established by peaceful Dravidians. Talk about "War as father of all things."

The fairytale of the superior patriarchy

Historical theories can only be verified by supportive written documents, which means that, since we are only able to read writings of the last 5000 years, patriarchal propaganda has been the only accepted witness of the past. Writings of the losing side, take the Carthaginians or Indus Dravidians for example, were destroyed in order to uphold the heroic epics spun by Romans and Indian Aryans. Incan script was outright denied, Europeans being unable to conceive that an advanced textile based culture of the Andes would write with string.

The perceived advantage of modern science is founded in its use of average sampling, which is supposed to accurately mirror reality. This is not true when looking at historical, social, and cultural sciences. 90% of possible samples of 90% of all cultures were destroyed before science even existed. Christianity was highly efficient at destroying anything related to "heathens", consequently we don't even know how Incas were able to build their Earthquake-proof cyclopic walls. Anything left by padres and conquistadors was destroyed by European colonial powers, which were convinced of the inferiority of anything non-European until decolonization. Artifacts of "primitive" cultures were good for nothing but the kings' collections of curiosities. Naturally, all views on foreign peoples were euro-centrally distorted until the 20th century.

The restricted sampling of victors over the last 5000 years portrayed history as a succession of victorious battles. Only two historians have received the Nobel prize: Theodor Mommsen for his Roman History, and Winston Churchill for his History of the Second World War.

This paved the way for propaganda of the superiors. War and power were unavoidable. If Hitler had won the war, Joseph Goebbels would still be editing German historiography. We would still believe in the superiority of the Aryan race, just as the U.S. Americans are still convinced of their divine destiny as the world's greatest nation, a view naturally contested by Arabs and Latin-Americans.

History is written by the victor, therefore all alternative narratives were eliminated. Yet, alternative theses push for progress. The alternative of male writing of history is the female perspective, but women had no say until the 1970s, and little has changed. Although they are allowed to study at universities, a professorship is only possible after internalizing patriarchal premises and publishing in a way acceptable to male department heads.

The historians' premise is a circular argument. The patriarchy has always existed, therefore all findings were developed by the patriarchy. Any contradicting artifacts are worthless, unscientific, and are hushed up or reinterpreted.

Circular reasoning is the opposite of science. Logic, as a partial discipline of philosophy, defeated the ecclesiastical dogma with this insight. Prior to Galileo Galilei's imprisonment the Church claimed that God created the world and dictated the Bible to humankind, therefore anything contradicting the Bible was nonsense and dangerous heresy. Simplified: God created the world, therefore only God can explain it. Even more simplified: The world is God's, therefore the world is God's. This is a classic tautology, saying everything and nothing.

This may seem ridiculous to us now, but it dominated the thought of the Western world for 1200 years. Nothing has really changed, except the omission of the word "God". We still think biblically. God being a man means history is male. Men have always ruled the world, therefore only men can rule the world.

Yet the premise that men have always ruled the world is very unlikely. Why? Since the 20th century, we have gained a good overview of human social orders.

80 years ago, ethnologists such as Margaret Mead, Claude Levi-Strauß, and Ruth Benedikt started to detail the social systems of surviving native peoples. They found a surprisingly great diversity: there are matrifocal, matrilineal, egalitarian, patrilineal, and patriarchal systems. This means there are roughly five different forms of human social structure, which were all equally probable and equally common prior to the short epoch of civilization. The probability of a patriarchal existence of Homo sapiens between 100,000 and 3300 BC is therefore a mere 20%.

In other words: There is an 80% probability that the world was not ruled by the patriarchy prior to deciphered Mesopotamian and Egyptian writings. This is reinforced by findings from prehistory, most of which point toward female oriented parent cultures.

When historians protest the female thesis for lack of evidence, then all fantasies of the great prehistoric hunter are similarly lacking. However, if mammoth bones are enough proof for successful male hunters, the many maternal statues have to be valid proof for a female social and religious strength.

War is the beginning of the end

I am frequently surprised at how the historical sciences could ignore their own greatest genius. Toynbee's Universal history provides answers to all those questions, which historians continue to ask over and over, as if there had not yet been an answer.

Toynbee published his 12 volume work "A Study of History"

between 1934 and 1961. It delineated a succession of steps identifiable in all then-known civilizations, about 1000 – 1200 years in duration, and consisting of two parts. (Rise and Downfall)

Cultures are creative and expand peacefully during the first centuries, in which neighboring peoples eagerly adapt their inventions and innovations. The ancient Greeks enjoyed this period from 800 to 480 BC, spreading their culture across the entire Mediterranean and Black Sea region.

Once creativity stagnates, the civilization splits into parties, fighting over the now limited possessions. Should there furthermore emerge an external threat, civil war and a militant dictatorship will follow, plunging the surrounding regions into war. From 480 BC on, Greece was threatened by the Persian empire and tore itself apart in the Peloponnese war. The military empires of Athens, Alexander the Great, and eventually the Romans were based on bellicose expansion. This warlike way is the beginning of the end, the traumatized Barbarian peoples will arm themselves and invasions will ultimately destroy the empire. The writing of history flourishes during this late, second stage of the empire, in order to justify high cost of violence, war, and traumatization.

Toynbee's law is simple enough to apply to every known war. Europe, for example, militarized in response to the perceived threat of the Islamic world, and tore itself to pieces in the reformation conflicts. Ultimately, absolutistic European kings turned the rest of the world into European colonies, and the resulting two world wars lead the European supremacy to collapse like collective suicide.

I have wondered since 1970, why historians continue to suppress or trivialize this simple truth. Toynbee's universal law has disproven the notion of the significance of military strength 80 years ago. It sets the following premises for the last 5000 years:

Cultural growth originates in times of peace.

Military power will expand for a while, but loses all legitimacy through violence and cruelty and will ultimately implode.

War was, is, and always will be the beginning of the downfall.

Senseless tyranny

I grew up at a time in which strong dictators were still said to have done some good, being able to act more efficiently than democrats. It may seem that way at the beginning of their reign, but ultimately they only bring destruction. The crueler they are, the quicker they fall:

The following law of violence has been universally applicable for 6000 years:

A ruler's cruelty and the duration of their rule are indirectly proportional, meaning a more brutal tyrant leads to a faster collapse of his empire:

Pol Pot: 4 years from Killing Fields until his banishment by the Vietnamese

Hitler: 12 years from his rise to power until collapse

Caesar: 15 years from the invasion of Gaul until his assassination

Napoleon: 16 years from rise to sole power until Waterloo

Winston Churchill: 20 years from rejecting the armistice (1940) until the fall of the British Empire (1960)

Stalin: 26 years from Trotzki's elimination until destalinization

Mao: 28 years from civil war victory until demaoization by Teng Siao Ping

Philipp II. Of Spain: 32 years from coronation until the fall of the great armada

These insights are not easy to digest for rulers and dictators. Once the people are aware of the truth, revolution will follow, usually meaning overthrow and death for the dictator. To counteract this, rulers use corruption and feudal systems to create a monopoly of wealth, allowing them to employ lobbyists and scholars to spread misinformation to keep the people ignorant. This has been done throughout the existence of government.

In this respect, the bellicose patriarchy of the last 6000 years is an aberration, leading to repeated traumatizing of the world's peoples.

According to Yuval Harari, expansive military power has only one positive impact: It creates steadily larger nations and encourages globalization. The fact that hostile nations are left in the dirt is accepted as collateral damage.

This advantage has disappeared since the completion of globalization in the 21st century. In this age of global economic and ecological interdependence, collateral damage affects every nation the same. If war induced traumatization is not dealt with and disposed of, the whole planet will face its downfall by 2100.

Do we really want to risk total loss, just because the patriarchy is supposedly great?

III. Genocides by the patriarchy

The Indo-Europeans

The patriarchy developed around 4500 BC in the southern Russian steppe. (Schmöckel 2015, Gimbutas 2010) Climate change dried up the fertile loess soil, and the indigenous Indo-Europeans began livestock farming (cattle and horses) This was a man's business and justified male supremacy. Some herds were allowed to grow through coincidences in climate. Their owners then ascended toward chieftains and ultimately kings.

The men protecting herds became combative because livestock was prone to theft. (We can still see this in the 19th century; most US Westerns pictured heroic cowboys fending off thieving bandits.) Wars were waged for herds, and chieftains gained power.

Aridity forced young people to move West in search of fresh pastures for their stock. As they invaded the surrounding areas, they showed no consideration for the native peoples, subjugated them and forced them to adopt the Indo-European language. In the wake of the Indo-European languages can be found an upper class Indo-European warrior caste, and a lower class native population. This is possible because the matrifocal lower class was potentially strictly pacifist. Once the subjugated women had been impregnated by the Indo-Europeans, they accept their fate out of love for their children, for which they are despised by their lords.

Around 3000 BC, the Indo-Europeans were ruling the Linear Pottery culture in Central Europe, around 2000 BC they had conquered the Danube culture and the rest of the Balkans. At the same time, Indo-European Hittites conquered Asia Minor and established the first major "Aryan" empire, lasting until 1200 BC. It was destroyed by the next wave of Indo-European invasions, which saw the defeat of the Mycenes, who had earlier bested the Minoans for naval supremacy in the Mediterranean.

The migration period of the 12th century BC ended with a Indo-European eastern Central Europe, and started a domino effect of migrations. The Celts went West, the Teutons occupied Scandinavia, the Italic people occupied Lazio and Umbria, the Dorians invaded Greece, and the Thracians moved into Asia Minor. From then on, Indo-Europeans were rulers of the Mediterranean region.

The unrestrained advance of these warring nomads was possible due to their advanced weaponry. They used metallurgy, taken from the Danube culture, to forge copper weapons, later on advancing to bronze weapons. Smelting bronze created the need for a Europe-wide trade of copper and tin, leading the Indo-Europeans to create horse drawn wagons, able to transport the heavy ores over long distances. Shortly after they realized they would be able to move at horse's speed with two-wheeled carriages. The chariot came to be the elite weapon of the Bronze Age. Once all advanced civilizations of the Middle East had implemented chariot regiments into their armies, the peoples of the steppes learned to ride horses and became even more agile. The cavalry was the deadliest offensive unit until the development of the tank in 1916. European colonial powers refined warfare with cannons and artillery, conquering the entire world.

Asia

In Kazakhstan, the eastern branch of Indo-Europeans perfected the chariot around 2000 BC, and spread across Central Asia. They invaded Persia and India and subjugated the old cultures in 1500 BC. As the Mitanni people they defeated the Hittites, Assyrians, and Babylonians. As the Medes and Persians they conquered the Middle East starting in 600 BC. Kyros the Great established history's first empire, lasting 220 years until being replaced by the Indo-European Greeks and Alexander the Great.

The Aryan invasion of India around 1500 BC led to serious consequences. The peaceful Dravidians stood no chance against the chariots, and all of northern India was soon ruled by Aryan kings.

The new rulers introduced segregation and turned oppression of the indigenous population into a religious system. Aryan kings and priests constituted the highest caste, the Brahmin, which to this day exhibits the light skin of the Indo-Europeans. All subordinated peoples, with light brown to dark brown skin, were divided into various lower castes. The Untouchables, the lowest in this strict caste hierarchy, were without rights altogether. This system is still responsible for India's incredible poverty, although there has lately emerged a rising middle class.

India has been getting torn apart by its matrifocal and patriarchal heritage for 3500 years.

Matrifocal culture survived within spirituality, retaining the Goddess of reincarnation and developing the Karma teachings, the world's leading spiritual explanation system. Buddha created the first religion of peace, which rejects the killing of animals and stayed true to its pacifist core. Christianity on the other hand allowed itself to be corrupted by Roman emperors.

The matrifocal elements of peace in India are strong enough to encourage a matrifocal restoration, had the patriarchy not repeatedly invaded the subcontinent. Starting in 500 BC, first Dareios and the Persians seized the Indus Valley, followed by Alexander and the Greeks, then the Bactrian Greeks, the Saka, the Huns, and the Kushans. After a brief interval of Kushan empire and Gupta empire rule, the Muslims arrived. Arabs first, followed by Persians, Afghans, and Mongols (Mogul empire). The 1000 year long oppression by patriarchal Islam eradicated Indian Buddhism. Repercussions can still be seen in wars between India and Pakistan, as well as Jihadist attacks.

To top it off, the British arrived in 1750, exploiting India and destroying its high-quality textile industry. India went from contributing 20% of the gross world product to only a few percent, in addition to suffering from famine.

We're left with China. The patriarchal founders of the Chinese empire were taught the art of war by the Indo-European Tocharians, who spread the use of chariot and cavalry in present-day Xinjiang Uyghur between 2000 BC and 500 AD. (Bott 2014) The Shang dynasty were keeping contact with the Tocharians, and the Zhou were in control of the area between China and Xinjiang before establishing the second dynastic empire. The Qin, Yuan, and Qing emperors were descendants of mongolian conquerors, who had adopted the use of cavalry from the Tocharians (called Yue Chi) and in turn defeated them around the time of the birth of Christ. The Yue Chi went on to establish the Kushan empire reaching from Xinjiang to Pakistan. The Warring States period (475 - 221 BC) ensued, until Shi Huang Di emerged victorious and ascended to be unified China's first emperor. Ultimately, even though China and the West are viewed as polar opposites, they share a patriarchal root in the Tocharians.

China continues to be a unified empire due to its geographical isolation, and has experienced more times of peace than India and Europe. Although it began worldwide seafaring before the Europeans, China never became a colonial power and had little interest in imperialism. The threat of the horsemen horde from the North was more important than ruling the Indian Ocean. Consequently, the Ming emperor had the Zheng He era armada burned, and chose to rebuild the Great Wall instead.

Africa

Eastern and southern Africa were inhabited by Khoisan-speaking natives until 1000 BC, their small tribes were organized in an egalitarian manner. The San and Khoikhoi in southwest Africa still live in this way. They are the last remnant of the once nomadic race, wandering about Homo sapien's cradle, from Ethiopia to South Africa.

The peoples inhabiting sub-Saharan Africa today originated in western Africa between Senegal and Nigeria as a result of adaptation to the west African jungle. Starting in 3000 BC, others came from the North: From 8000 to 4000 BC, the Sahara was fertile countryside, a paradise for humans and animals with an abundance of food and water. Cattle herders established themselves there, but had to move south as the desert expanded. This led to conflict over diminishing grazing lands. The Garamantes (present-day Tuareg) left Syria around 800 BC and settled in the Sahara oases, becoming a trade junction between North and South. They also brought innovations of civilizations to Nigeria, foremost agriculture and iron smelting. The primordial culture of the Bantu developed around in eastern Nigeria around 1000 BC, and by 800 BC it had learned how to manufacture iron and iron weaponry.

As population pressure rose in Nigeria, the only option was to head east. In the North was the desert, South the ocean, and West other large tribes made expansion impossible. Bantu tribes settled Africa from the Sahara to Cape Province over the next 2000 years. All Bantu languages originate from primordial Bantu, spoken in a small part of Southeastern Nigeria.

How could this happen?

After adopting agriculture, livestock breeding, and iron weaponry from the North, the primordial Bantu started to reorganize in a patriarchal manner. They sent expeditions to the East and South, where the Khoisan stood no chance against the invaders. The Khoisan fled to the jungle and the Kalahari desert. Furthermore, Semites from Yemen invaded Ethiopia, overran the local Khoisan and integrated the remainder into a shared gene pool.

Patriarchy in Africa developed through acculturation of Northern customs. Tribes enslaved each other as a result of a lucrative slave trade established by the Arabs in the East, and the Portuguese in the West. Once slavery becomes commonplace, the objectification of women follows. The Pharaonic circumcision was a ritual of oppression and abuse. Countless young men became Eunuchs in the harems of Cairo, Baghdad, and Istanbul, or the plantations of the Caribbean, Brazil, and Southern USA.

In spite of this history of violence, rich kingdoms arose in the Sahel region. (Fauvelle 2017) The largest, Mali, was bigger than Charlemagne's France, and its King Mansa Musa was indescribably wealthy. The kingdoms of the Sahel region were all involved in trade in the Islamic world, and became rich in the process.

Then the Europeans arrived.

After 1500 AD, depopulation was a growing problem as a result of the Portuguese and British slave trade. Starting in 1880, the entire continent was being colonized and exploited. King Leopold II of Belgium was the cruelest of the oppressors. In only a few decades he decimated his "private property" in Belgian Congo to such a degree, its population dropped from 20 million to 10 million. Today's warlords are nothing compared to the brutality of the Belgian colonial administration, which even had small children's hands and feet mutilated. Violence in Congo still is a result of these past atrocities.

Before, and after most African countries gained independence during Decolonization in 1960, there has been an alliance between European and African patriarchies, suppressing the continent's chances for development. African patriarchs became assistants to European oppressors and continue being such. As long as they supply the needed resources for the United States and Europe, they are free to exploit their own population to enrich themselves. (Seitz 2018) This extreme exploitation is inhibiting any chance of progress for the African population. African countries need to realize their strengths and cast out the despots.

Oppression and eradication

The patriarchal global conquest has always been using genocides to spread terror and force compliance. (Naimark 2018) In the Old Testament, a punitive God demands the killing of the Holy Land's population because they worshiped a wrong God. This provided the ideological blueprint for genocides over the last 3000 years. The

Greeks killed the Trojans, and all island and city dwellers of adversary allegiance during the Peloponnesian War. The Romans enslaved the Carthaginians along with all other defeated peoples. The Mongolian empire, the largest empire in history, was based on the genocide of conquered peoples, which would cause panic and led to the voluntary surrender of future enemies. China and Persia was overrun by Genghis Khan and his horsemen. "Christian" crusaders did the same in Palestine, Southern France and the eastern territories of Germany. In the 16th century, the Spaniards killed 90% of the 80 million Indians, who were forced to labor without sufficient food and water and died of typhus and smallpox. In the USA, Australia and South Africa, settlers eradicated the native populations and took their land. Then there are the genocides of communist dictators and national socialists. Naimark unmasks the particulars of mass killing and deconstructs the euphemized or embellished narrative. Denouncing enemies and natives as primitive and godless subhumans establishes the universal foundation for greed, stealing land, and massacres.

How can man be capable of such cruelty? Biology provides an answer: All beast of prey kill rivals and their offspring in a fight for limited food sources of their region. Man is the most efficient predator of all time, resulting in extreme ways of fighting for food and land.

Ferretti (2017) has statistically recorded the warlike incidents of the last 4000 years, in order to understand the causes of wars. He draws the conclusion that war and violence are used to perpetuate the interests of social constructs (states, religions, ideologies), being expansion and stabilization of their territories. States are social organisms with an average lifespan of 300 years, until being defeated or destroyed by successor states. The life of an individual is unimportant, moreover thousands of individuals are sacrificed for the preservation of the social construct. Looking at 5400 historically recorded war, Ferretti calculates a constant ratio of 1 violent conflict per 1 million humans and century. This means the number of violent incidents increased proportional to population growth.

There are two exceptions: The violence ratio decreased during the time of Pax Romana (stabile empires were also present in China, Persia, India, and Central America). Secondly, violence has decreased since 1950, the most significant globalization period with worldwide trade and nuclear deterrence. This brings me to the conclusion that war as a means of politics will become obsolete once territorial stability is warranted through other means (trade, economy, diplomacy). This amicable tendency can be observed as being timeless (Buddha, Laozi, Pythagoras, Christ, Pelagius). Since 1947, nonviolent communication has been on the rise (Gandhi, Martin Luther King, Mandela, UN conferences, international treaties) because the costs of warfare have significantly exceeded the spoils for a long while now.

Haarmann (2002) has knowledge of all languages of the past. Extinct languages are like a genetic fingerprint. Sound shifts allow us to trace which languages are related or originate from another. Borrowed words reflect the cultural relationships of the past. Empires such as the Romans eradicated most languages of integrated peoples through acculturation. In the 20th century, this process has accelerated due to globalisation. The bloody trail of the patriarchy can be identified in the insights of linguists. Most of the world's languages are extinct to a point of not even spawning a successor language, which could be used to trace back to the original. The suppression of languages spoken by minorities is in the interest of the powerful. Once the native speakers are exterminated, their culture disappears, and with it all memory of the genocide responsible for its extinction.

War in the Middle Ages

European medieval culture originated in Irish and Frankish abbeys, which stood for nonviolence and established peaceful trade networks in the free cities. At the same time, Europe was threatened by vikings, Hungarians, and Saracens, and the resulting militarization led to the terrifying cruelty of European powers. Furthermore, Europe's long tradition of war (being the first country conquered by kurgan warriors) plays a significant role in the rise of the most atrocious patriarchy in history.

Althoff (2017) addresses warfare between 500 and 1500 AD, and overthrows any romanticized fantasies of noble knights. He describes the Middle Ages as a dreadful time ruled by a brutal warrior caste, declaring war and feuds at any time against anyone, plundering vast areas, and killing fellow statesmen. Chivalry was reserved for members of the knighthood, who were captured for ransom. These extortions led to impoverishment of entire families as well as power shifts, one such example being Richard Lionheart, whose ransom paid for various Austrian strongholds. Farmers, craftsmen, and townsfolk were pawns for the mighty, were sacrificed, tortured, raped, robbed, or killed. The fragmentation of Europe led to an endless series of wars, in which warfare was perfected. At this point, Europe was superior to all other countries. The contradiction of Christianity and violence was reasoned away by the introduction of the "just war" concept by church father Augustinus. Violence against heathens and heretics was justified per se and was legitimized as a crusade by the pope. Thus the raids of the Baltic States by the German Order, including the eradication of Baltic Prussians, were presented as conversion of the heathens, when in truth they were an early form of colonialism.

As a child I was excited about knights and castles. I now know this was due to the transfigured myths of our former oppressors, stories that were further inflated by the nationalism of the 19th century. After reading Althoff's book, noble knights make me feel nothing but disgust.

Genocide in the Muslim world

From 635 AD on, muslim Arabs conquered the Middle East, northern Africa, and Spain. Since then they have been denounced as bloodthirsty heathens in Europe. The conquered land had to be taken back.

The truth is different. The Arab expansion was a reaction to centuries of wars between Persia and Byzantium, with Arab tribes caught in the middle. The caliphate was only able to survive over centuries by being tolerant with Christian and Jewish subordinates, even improving the female status. Nobody was forcibly converted, the lost peace of the Roman empire was restored, Jews and Christian Armenians got rich in trade, mystic Sufi orders preached love and reconciliation, and Arabic science and literature were at the forefront worldwide.

The time of peace was interrupted by invading Turkish Seljuks and the "Christian" crusaders between 1071 and 1299. The brutality with which crusaders slaughtered Jerusalem's entire population ("wading knee-deep in the blood of their enemies") traumatized the Arab world, and can still be identified as a factor in the Palestine conflict. Even worse were the Mongolian invasions starting in 1240. City populations were eradicated if they did not surrender right away. The conquered were trampled by horses and their skulls piled up into pyramids. Persians were the main victims of the mass murders, resulting in a radicalization of the Shi'ah.

Islamic unity was reestablished by the Ottoman empire starting in 1500 AD. 300 years of internal peace followed, until Europeans decided to try and subjugate the last remaining independent, non-Christian empire. In the 19th century, England, France, and Russia little by little colonized Algeria, Tunisia, Morocco, Egypt, Suda, Caucasus, and Central Asia. World War I was truthfully a final battle waged by colonial powers fighting for the last scraps. Syria, Lebanon, Iraq, and Palestine have had to pay for this madness until today.

Before Arabia had time to recuperate from this trauma, the USA found oil in Saudi Arabia in 1938. They established a neocolonial oil empire, toppled the democratically elected Persian government in 1953, and plunged Iraq, Afghanistan, and Libya into war starting in 1991. Israel was chosen to fight various proxy wars. The US strategy to enable "regime changes" in order to instate US-friendly marionettes failed in all these countries (including Yemen), making them "failed states".

Increasing traumas during this period of colonialism and neocolonialism led to increased radicalization of resistance groups. Jihadism is a response to US interference, who therefore bred their terrorist threat themselves (Osama Bin Laden and Saddam Hussein were initially financed by the CIA). Lüders documented these processes in his writings. (Lüders 2018)

The USA are now producing enough oil for themselves, and are leaving the Middle East. Their allies are stuck with cleaning up the shambles left behind by the US military.

The destruction of America

The biggest civilization catastrophe was the discovery of America by Columbus (Mann 2016, Rinke 2019), at least from the Native American perspective. There were 80 million Natives in 1492, and their cities bigger, their crops more nourishing than any cities or crops in the Old World. Nothing has changed today: corn, pumpkin, tomatoes, beans, potatoes, cacao, manioc; all of it comes from millenia of growing and breeding by Native Americans. 90% of their population died within 30 years from diseases like smallpox and measles, against which their immune system was not prepared. Vegetable fields of North America and the Amazon region became fallow. While Orellana had described flourishing cities around the discovery of the Amazon, the next explorer met nobody. The Terra Preta of the rivers is a witness to the advanced horticulture of the area. Any survivors of the smallpox were taken care of by Cortez and Pizarro. Tenochtitlan was destroyed, and the Incan gold was melted down. An enormous body of knowledge was lost. Aztec books were burned, and only a fraction was reconstructed. The art of cyclopean masonry was lost forever.

The Natives were decimated by sickness and oppression, their culture and knowledge stolen, until finally they were viewed as savages whose murder was just. The true savages were us

Europeans. The Aztecs, instead of killing their enemies on the battlefield, took them prisoner to be sacrificed to the Gods. Before 1492, wars in Mexico were far less bloody than anything that followed.

Before we can realize the true magnitude of the destruction of America, we have to come to terms with the sham fed to us by Catholicism that we've been civilizing Latin America for the last 500 years. This is a brazen lie. In 1519, Tenochtitlan was the most splendid city on Earth. It was destroyed two years later. In 1533, the Inca empire was the most efficiently organised empire in the world, comparable to the Roman empire. In only a few years, the Spaniards lay waste to it. The oppression of a native and mestizo majority by a small white minority has continued for 500 years. The conditions established by Spain and Portugal have been perpetuated by the USA through military interventions, CIA coups, and multinational company interests since 1898. It will take centuries of pain and tears for America to recover from the violence of Europe.

The only good Indian is a dead Indian

Who doesn't hear this proverb and think of noble Indian Winnetou, who we followed and rooted for to protect his native land in Karl May's books about the Wild West?

Seemingly only Germans, for who the USA was a far away land. The Americans on the other hand were serious about the proverb, and their Westerns portray Native Americans as the bad guys. The Wild West is "saved" by the cavalry. Finally in 1990, Kevin Kostner put himself into the place of Natives in the movie "Dances with Wolves".

The US cavalry eradicated 95% of natives in order to take their land and give it to white settlers. Of two million Natives, only 20,000 to 30,000 survived the American Indian Wars. This number has again increased to two million, but the Natives will never regain their lands and culture.

Whites justified the countless massacres by identifying the uncivilized brutality of the Indians, who martyred prisoners at the stake and scalped them. At the same time, scalping was facilitated by English governors, who would pay for scalps of slain Indians, no matter if man, woman, or child. The stake was a trial of courage, through which captured enemies could earn respect.

Historians excuse the behavior of Whites by pointing out the warring nature of Prairie Indians. Natives would kill each other, which was stopped by civilization. There's one thing which is not mentioned: There were peaceful Native realms in the Mississippi basin as well as the Southeast and Southwest of the USA. They originated in a time before Columbus, and established mighty mounds, great Pueblo cities, and fertile fields. The Spanish discoverer De Soto spoke of enormous cities in southeastern USA.

From 1519 on, Spaniards invaded Mexico and the entire South of the United States, from Florida to California, subjecting all to genocide. The key weapon was the cavalry, which was as foreign to the Natives as the horse. Prairie Indian spent time until 1800 stealing horses and adopting the mounted warrior practice. They used this superior weapon of the Whites to raid and conquer other tribes. The warlike Prairie Indians are therefore a consequence of genocide by the Spanish. There were border skirmishes before Columbus's arrival, but it was mostly a chance for young men to prove their courage, never a fight to conquer the other tribe. The first conquered people were the Hurons, who became part of the Iroquois. The conquerors were a matriarchal nation with a parliament, and were taught warfare by the English and Dutch after an insatiable demand for beaver skins had incited Natives against each other.

Protests of the late 1960 were instigated by American hippies, who showed solidarity with Natives and admired their peaceful contact with nature. The hippie movement spawned the ecological movement, a late victory for the native religion of Mother Earth.

Colonialism, Imperialism, and Neocolonialism

The Europeans conquered the globe from 1492 on. (Reinhard 2016) Reinhard shows us who we are, where we are from, and where we are going. 600 years ago, we made up a small part on the fringes of the world, bystanders to the flourishing life happening in the Middle East, India, and China. Times changed! The entire world came to know and fear us. We colonized and subjugated most of the world, and our cultural and economic structures are as universally engrained as always.

The Greeks conquered Asia in antiquity. Bactrian Greeks established kingdoms in India, and Greek art travelled the Silk Road to China. The Portuguese circumnavigated Africa and seized control of Asian maritime trade. The Dutch, French, and English followed suit. Spaniards circumnavigate the Earth and establish the first global trade network. Silver is transported from the mines of Potosí via the Philippines to China; silk is transported to Europe. The English amass riches with the slave trade and exploit India.

Traces of the global conquest are apparent worldwide. Afonso de Albuquerque shelled the coastal cities of India and Persia, and expelled Arabs from the spice trade. The Dutch conquered Java and the Molucca Islands, turning a huge profit from trading pepper and tulips. Holland was at the center of 17th century global trade, and a seemingly insignificant thing, the tulip bulb, is the main factor leading to a market crash in Amsterdam. Meanwhile, Spaniards were enslaving all indigenous peoples of Latin America. Portugal and Brazil were doing similar things: After running out of Native American slaves, they carry Africans from Angola and Mozambique across the Atlantic. The African slaves have higher endurance, already being accustomed to the epidemics of the Old Worlds. At first, the English compete against the Portuguese for slaves, but abolish slavery in the 19th century after realizing they could satisfactorily exploit their colonies nonetheless. In 1920, England rules a quarter of world and its population.

Once the colonized peoples start showing resistance, the

maintenance or retention of the colonies becomes increasingly expensive. Decolonization gaines momentum in 1947, still the economic dependence endures, is perhaps getting stronger. london, Antwerp, and New York are still controlling the flow of trade goods and wealth today.

The European imperialistic mode of life expanded globally during the 20th century. (Brand 2017) In 1991, capitalism won the Cold War, and mass media celebrates the imminent rescue of the world through economic growth. Political and economic committees has since unquestionably adopted the premises of capitalist economy, criticism of which is attributed to non-parliamentarian NGOs. Pointing out the relation of exploiting the planet and exploiting humans is branded as eco-craze. Even communist China is ascending to being leader of global capitalism.

Achieving worldwide opinion leadership is the nature of capitalism, but does not solve any problems. The invisible arm of the market is by no means a universal regulator, but only clears the way for unscrupulous enrichment of the few already rich. The ones who are well off ensure their high standard of living by paying no regard to nature and the exploited population. The suitor, able to choose from many beautiful women at a brothel, does not lose sleep over exploiting sex slaves, who were violently forced into prostitution. The teenager, able to buy cheap clothes, does not think about labor slaves in Bangladesh, who work in cramped factories under constant threat of being trapped by fire. The husband, bringing home roses for his wife to show his love, does not think about workers in Ecuador, who are poisoned by pesticides. Global wealth rises, and a growing middle class is established. The exploitation of the lower class stays the same. This begs the question, if consideration for the well being of fellow human beings is as low as it seems, how bad is it for animals and plants?

Any cigarette smoker in Europe has to look at pictures of bronchial carcinoma on their cigarette pack every time they reach for another. By that logic, consumers of meat and palm oil should have to look at recordings of slaughterhouses, charred animals, and trees in cleared jungles. The imperialistic way of life without consideration for losses has to stop. Humans have survived for 300,000 years without consuming more than what nature provided. Sociologists claim that life with nature leads to more happiness than the race for commodities and goods, a capitalistic false ideal. The alternative works: On the beach of Dakar in Senegal, hundreds of people are active in sport. They are happy, form friendships, and stay in shape. For this, they do not spend a single cent, thus according to capitalistic criteria they are worthless. They are contributing to the Gross National Happiness (GNH), which, for example, has been central to Bhutan's governmental mission since the 18th century.

Political scientist Seville (2018) criticizes the decline of political speech. A true discussion of Pro and Con, of visions, advantages, disadvantages, and consequences leading to a collective solution has become rare. The expertocracy pretending to know the singular truth does not understand the population. Neoliberal national economy claims possession of the one true economic method and insight, and deflects any objections. The neoliberal theory is an ideology which pushes money from the bottom up and benefits the rich. (Schulmeister 2018) The neoliberal countermovement against the Keynesians works with suggestive textbook arrangements as well as manipulative pictures and graphics, presented as truth, without any of their frameworks being based on empirical data. Fortunately, the mass public has become aware of embellished phrases spewed by the economic-commercial cartel, and sees that reality is different than what the words and actions of politicians and economist would make it seem. (Pahl 2017)

Global corporations are outside of democratic control, pay no taxes, destroy the environment, use tax payers to pay for the damage they create; they employ lobbyists, journalists, and scientists to influence the global mindset for their own profit. (Bode 2018) Climate change would not be a problem anymore if it weren't for the continued resistance of coal, oil, and automobile industries. VW and its consorts do not care about the Diesel Lie, they pay a low fine and keep on poisoning the public with nitrogen oxide and particulate matter. Banks are enormous money redistribution machines, profiting the wealthy. Goldman-Sachs dominates US government and operates as if the bank scandal had never happened. (Debts caused by banks are paid off by the public through inflation, tax raises, expensive apartments, and minimal to no savings interest rates). Corporations either destroy democracy or manipulate it to further their own interest. The only defence against this are liability laws, protecting individual damages as well as common welfare. Damages caused by profit focused corporations can be kept in check, as for example with the tobacco industry, but presently legal, destructive business models have to become illegal for our children to live in a world for humans, not for profit.

The powerful sit in skyscrapers, ruling the financial and economic markets, create the Boni out of thin air to buy out the rest of the world, and beat down competitors by socializing debt and through negative interest, lease price, and national bankruptcies. Their ancestors used horses and called themselves knights. Nowadays, computers are way more efficient. Neoliberalism tries to convince the public that it's best for everyone if the wealthy get richer. Objections are silenced by the poverty trap. Continuing unrest is solved by corruption of entire nations (Venezuela, Haiti, Simbabwe, Congo).

Controlling the market makes destroying the Earth easier. For one who's feet are not on the ground but on the top floor of a skyscraper, ecology must be a foreign subject, and nature out of touch. To stop ordering the destruction of entire ecosystems with the stroke of a pen, they would have to leave their bubble of virtual monetary values every once in a while.

Modern nomadic invasions

Modern civilization's powerful find the idea of their methods tracing back to primitive nomads laughable.

The discoverer of the Indo-European patriarchy, Marija Gimbutas, was maliciously diminished, in spite of being a highly decorated

Harvard professor. They pointed out, if Gimbutas claimed that the mighty patriarchy descended from Indo-Europeans, she would make Hitler's idea of the Aryan Übermensch reputable again. The opposite is true: Gimbutas unveiled the intrinsic fascist behavior of authoritarian ideas, which was laid bare for the public especially defined in Hitler's delusions of grandeur. Gimbutas lead the fairytale of Indo-European centered civilizing progress ad absurdum. (Bott 2014)

The ridiculous argument exists that someone who cautions against fascism, is a fascist themselves. Sounds absurd, but it has been used throughout history:

The protestants identified Rome as the Babylon of the Apocalypse, and Pope Alexander VI as the Antichrist. This sentiment was turned against them immediately: Whoever spoke of the Devil, or recognized the evil present in Cesare Borgia's actions, had to have been aligned with the Devil. Protestants were burned at the stake as heretics. Today the word heretic is substituted by "conspiracy theorist".

Looking closely, the theory of nomadic livestock farming leading to patriarchal authoritarian thought can be seen as highly topical. Even in modern times the largest empires were founded by nomads, fighting over stock and influencing corrupt sham democracies with bought out voter-stock.

Toynbee deals with the Ottoman empire, the largest empire on European soil in the modern age. The Ottomans were Turkish nomads from Central Asia, who had conquered the entire Byzantine empire, the Balkans, Egypt, Mesopotamia, the coast of the Black Sea, the Caucasus, Tunisia, and more. They had driven Christianity in Europe to the brink of extinction by 1683. Sultans thought and acted like nomads in fancy clothes. The subjugated peoples were moved around like cattle herds within the empire. They were bred like cattle, and children taken from their mothers to be child soldiers.

"That's how they are, the Moslems", one might think and feel themselves morally superior. Yet the nomadic authoritarian idea transcends religion and nation borders. All large, modern age empires were founded by nomads. The biggest empire in history was established by Mongolian Genghis Khan. The Mogul empire in India was founded by Mongolian nomads, the Chinese Manchu empire (1644 - 1911) by Tungusic nomads. They lasted until the English, French, and Germans arrived.

Well, perhaps that is the reason all these peoples fell into decadence and had to bow to European civilization and progress? In reality, Caucasians are especially influenced by nomadic methods.

Nomadism is not a traditional way of life and has nothing to do with the hunters and gatherers of primitive peoples. Nomadism originated in the northern reaches of the first agricultural communities due to a drought in Anatolia. In 6200 BC, agricultural farmers left Catal Huyuk after the ground turned barren, and headed north. (Bott 2014) Times of drought impact the ability to grow grain, but stinted grassland can still supports plenty of livestock for survival. This led to a fixation on quantity (capital) and livestock became money (lat. pecunia, from pecus - livestock).

The essence of patriarchal authority is treating humans like livestock, and we still do it. The thrill of power started with the conquest of speed (speed races are still men's favorite hobby). The domestication of the horse allowed men to adopt their speed, able to attack quickly and expand their rule over large areas. Horses were crucial in establishing large empires until 1914.

Europeans further developed the nomadic concept and discovered the utility of ships. They turned into sea nomads and used state-run piracy to conquer far away lands. Piracy back then was official: Kings issued letters of marque as a form of state sanctioned license to kill. Surprise attacks using ships enabled Europeans to devastate and plunder America, Africa, Asia, and Australia. Without piracy conducted by the East India Company, the British Empire would not have existed.

The USA took nomadic predation a step further. All rapid means of transport were used for expansion (horse, ship, tank, humvee, airplane, rockets, drones). The capitalist invasion of the world was further supported by neoliberal economic thought: wealth is good and exploitation promotes economic growth. More efficient than military conquest is economic expansion through hostile takeover of businesses and national economies.

Many US Americans define themselves as modern nomads and are deployed as such by corporations. To be able to advance in a multinational corporation, one has to be willing to change residence every few years, to other cities, countries, and continents. This is the only way to advance to the middle and upper management level.

In this way, modern nomads lose their connection to country, nature, and home. Their motto becomes "The world is my home". This is typical nomadic thought and originates from Indo-European horsemen settling in ever new lands.

Young, ambitious upward climbers may see this as exciting, but for subordinated farmers and workers it is less so. Alarm bells start ringing when corporate delegates from the US, England, and China arrive. They siphon off monetary value and close factories, leaving workers unemployed and suffering from precarity. The "restructurers" do not care about country and people because they'll be gone somewhere else within two or three years.

IV. The oppression of women

Women of subjugated peoples were not alone in their pain, as the patriarchy oppressed both male and female.

But, the oppression of women had double, even triple impact.

> 1. They were oppressed for being lower class, which meant dealing with hunger, poverty, and lack of rights. They shared this lot with the men, and fought for survival together. The facts on this were detailed in the last chapter.

> 2. They were oppressed for being female. Women lack all rights in a patriarchy, are unemployed and penniless, making them completely dependent on their husbands (men). I will describe the consequences of this actuality in the following chapter.

> 3. They are oppressed on a mental and moral level, by devaluing femininity and womanhood as fiendish, libidinous, foolish, or licentious. All female accomplishments are denied or stolen by men and presented as their own. The perfidiousness of this inversion of truth (Werlhof 2011) is shown in the next chapter.

Worldwide genocide of women

The most tragic consequence of depriving women of their rights is that it branded them as fair game for violence, murder, mutilation, and torture. We can still see this happening from violence in a marriage, rape, femicide, genital mutilation, Sati (widow burning), to the mutilation of feet (China until 1949).

The oppression of women under the patriarchy transformed into continuing genocide on a global scale. In order to wipe out hostile peoples, women were raped, kidnapped, or killed. This behavior has been present on all continents touched by the patriarchy for 6000 years. Clytemnestra cries her woe in the Greek saga of the Atreides, when Agamemnon is planning to sacrifice her daughter Iphigenia for the sake of the Trojan war: He had killed her husband and child, raped her soaked in the blood of her love ones - now he wanted to take her daughter! The myth is a account of the fate of Crete Minoans under conquest of the Greeks.

In the Middle Ages women were degraded to birthing machines for the breeding of soldiers. They were barred from education of any kind because the act of thinking was supposed to lead to a shrinkage of the uterus, endangering the purpose of the woman.

From 1450 to 1750 AD, the Catholic church extinguished female intelligence and understanding from Europe by targeting healers and midwives to be burned at the stake. The first bestseller of the Catholic church was the "Hammer of Witches", published in 1487, a manual for femicide presented as a treatise of witchcraft.

The burning of witches was predated by a general degradation of older women, summarized in a then common proverb: "Only the pyre for old crones." Being too old to bear children, they became scapegoats for any misfortunes. Even astronomer Johannes Kepler had to fight for six years (1615-1621) to save the life of his aged mother, who was sentenced to burn at the stake. (Rublack 2018)

The forbearance exhibited by "traditional" middle-class women was sheer fear for survival. Many developed mental problems, which was attributed to inflammation of the uterus (hysteria). Researching treatment for female hysteria led Sigmund Freud to uncover the system of sexual suppression, an eternal thorn in the paw of the patriarchy.

Many African peoples still practice female genital mutilation (FGM), first removing clitoris and inner labia, then sewing shut the vagina with unsterile needles. This guarantees the future husband a "pure" wife. This atrocity and its consequences has been detailed in Waris Dirie's books.

China is lacking women of an age suitable for marriage due to their practice of primarily aborting female fetuses over the last 40 years. The common practice of mutilating women's feet from birth on was only abolished under Mao Zedong in 1949.

Giving birth to a daughter is still considered a misfortune in India. Women are fair game for rape and murder, Sati - burning of widows - continues to exist, and the death of a female infant is nothing worth questioning. India is also slowly running out of marriageable women.

Family violence in Europe mostly targets women. Femicide is a daily occurence, and serial killers predominantly target women. Dangerous threats before and after divorces are only punished by the police after the woman has already been killed.

Is it surprising that many women are not on good terms with men?

Origin of the "bad mother"

200 years ago, 90% of European mothers were living in poverty and dependency, while nobles were enjoying their expensive appanage. Mothers had to join in the harvest and had to leave infants and toddlers behind, alone at home. Accidents or animal attacks led to injuries while the children were alone. Some mothers were sent to foreign cities for work, so their infants entered orphanages. Many died there. Charles Dickens turned this reality of hardship into world literature. (Morland 2019)

Until 200 years ago, giving birth was the duty of women. Midwives and wise women helped, weaving matrifocal knowledge and herbal medicine into obstetrics.

Men joined the field in the 19th century, and childbirth takes place in hospitals now. Gynecology was a male discipline until 30 years ago. Modern medicine has without doubt lowered child and mother fatality rates in the course of the 20th century.

This was long not the case. Medical students would examine women in childbed (post birth) and touch their vagina with dirty hands after having dissected a corpse, leading to widespread infection with cadaveric poison. Many of the women died. Ignaz Semmelweis identified childbed fever as an infection by cadaveric poison in 1847, and it took him a long time to implement necessary hygiene regulations. Leading physicians denied the correlation for decades, calling disinfection a waste of time. Rudolf Virchow even denied the iatrogenic connection in his medical textbook of 1896, after Semmelweis had proven a 10 times higher mortality rate in postpartum rooms visited by doctors who also had dissection duties elsewhere. The scandal was suppressed and Ignaz Semmels was assigned to a closed psychiatric department, where he died in 1865.

The medically induced childbed fever epidemic orphaned thousands of children, who were heavily traumatized by their mother's death. Most did not get placed with loving foster parents, and many ended up in homes or on farms, raised to be laborers. Untreated fear of abandonment is passed on to their children and grandchildren. Individuals suffering from depression nowadays can trace their fears to the loss of the good mother, passed down from generation to generation. Abandoned daughters grew to be emotionally numb "bad" mothers, having never experienced how a loving mother treats her children.

The collective orphan-trauma was intensified by the demographic turnaround of the 19th century. (Morland 2019) During the period of high postpartum mortality rates for mothers, a decrease of poverty due to industrialization led to a lower child mortality rate. German and Austrian mothers of the 19th century had up to ten children. In the early 19th century, children died and mothers lived. In the second half, it was the other way around. Many family histories show the following situation: five or six children survived after the mother died in childbirth (especially when switching from home birth to hospital birth). Losing one's mother became an epidemic, but was met with a disinterested shrug, just as the deaths of infants had been. A generation of traumatized daughters grew up to develop postpartum depression on having their first child, remembering the death of their own mother in their infancy. (Opelt 2008)

Sons who lost their mothers develop ambivalence towards women. They experience an unconscious compulsion to repeatedly leave the women they love, especially after the birth of their child. The men repress their trauma flashback while demonizing the loved one and fleeing in panic. Many women remember a loving relationship until pregnancy brought about a radical change of the partner. This change is misinterpreted as jealousy, when it is really the male counterpart of postpartum depression.

Loss of the mother has always been the biggest fear of the collective subconscious. Most popular and loved fairy tales portray dramatic consequences of losing the mother (Hansel and Gretel, Snow White, Cinderella). The deceased mother is replaced with the evil stepmother, who endeavors to make life miserable.

Modern medicine has reduced mother and child fatality rates to only a few per mill. We are now faced with a new problem. Fertility medicine will lead to an epidemic of anxious and insecure children suffering from behavioral problems and ADHD. Seeing Maria Arlamovsky's documentary "Future Baby", reporting on the extremes of fertility medicine, gave me nausea. Health professionals have no clue about the mental consequences of their field. I can get on board with simple insemination, if it enables childless mothers to have the child they desire. Emphasis on "if". The mental suffering of unsuccessfully treated women, who have to surrender after many expensive attempts at insemination, is left out of the picture. Better treatment would be to process the mental impact of women's suffering. Even muscle pumping macho Arnold Schwarzenegger was smart enough to start couples therapy with his wife Maria Shriver. It led to four naturally conceived children.

Childlessness is an unconscious protest against millenia of sexual oppression. Husbands need to realize this, that helping "infertile" women psychologically will lead to children conceived in the most extraordinary ways, perhaps abdominal pregnancy after having had a hysterectomy. Not too long ago, countless women were subjected to hysterectomies without reflection on the impact on their identity. Furthermore, 30 years ago physicians convinced thousands of women that they were infertile, leading to many unplanned pregnancies. My wife was one of them, and my stepson had to digest the consequences his whole childhood.

Then there is the madness of having three different mothers from three different countries act as ovum donor, pregnant mother, and adoptive mother. Adding sperm donor and adoptive father results in the kids carrying the heritage of five different parental lineage, three of which they do not know. Mental problems of the adopted children will take on a dimension beyond anything family constellations can treat.

Over the past few years the number of Caesareans has increased because artificial birth is easier for hospitals, and gynecologists do not want to risk being sued for damages resulting from childbirth. Lawyers on the other hand encourage these lawsuits, further increasing the number of C-sections. This has had evolutionary impact after only a few decades. The size of the birth canal is a compromise of erect gait and the baby's head size. This relation was optimized throughout human evolution to allow for natural birth.

Caesareans make this evolutionary correction obsolete, and an increasing number of women are born with pelvises too small for natural birth. They are entirely dependent on physicians and C-sections.

Postpartum depression

I had a strange experience at my doctoral defense in psychiatry/psychopathology, which at first I perceived as merely unjust, but have since come to understand its meaning.

The professor, who was head of the psychiatric clinic at the time, asked about the causes of postpartum depression. I answered according to the textbook and got an A. My female colleague went after me. The two of us had studied together for the exam. She factually provided the same answer, but, as an emancipated woman, let show a fragment of personal opinion. The professor got angry and kept digging, judging all of her answers as wrong. He wanted to hear that postpartum depression had biological causes, but she would not give in. Ultimately, he let her pass with a D.

What upset the professor so, it was only an exam?

I understand now. He was a member of the SS and had never moved past their biologistic idea of man. The cause of postpartum depression had to be biological, otherwise one had to reflect on the situation of the mother.

It is high time to do just that. Postpartum depression is a mental condition, resulting from traumatic experiences.

Postpartum depression is at first glance a repercussion of the childbed fever epidemic of the 19th century. Beyond that, if the mother-child-tie is violated before, during, or after birth, the subconscious of the daughter harbors a traumatic memory and unconscious fear of giving birth. This fear resurfaces during the first pregnancy and is affirmed by negative prognoses, amniocentesis, and unfriendliness. Women who have miscarriages are eagerly referred to fertility medicine because it is lucrative. The biological perspective leads women to develop insecurities about their ability to give birth and drives them to overeager C-sections.

The psychosocial situation of a mother in labor is just as significant. Being abandoned or threatened with abandonment by her partner, not knowing how to survive financially, having unsupportive parents and relatives for cultural reasons; all these factors will combine with the negative memory of her own birth. No wonder she suffers from depression.

Low class women have to deal with another real threat. More and more newborns are taken from poor and depressed mothers by child protective services. Postpartum depression is traditionally seen by the public authorities as the inability to love the child and sufficiently care for it. This leads to a vicious cycle: A woman, forcefully taken from her mother as an infant, suffers from postpartum depression due to unconscious memory of her personal trauma, resulting in her child being taken away. This leads to generations of mother child trauma, which is then erroneously interpreted as "genetic" by psychologists looking for biological cause.

We have to put a stop to this misguided development by remembering women's ancient, intuitive knowledge regarding the birthing process. Childbirth has to reclaim its matrifocal sanctity in order for mothers to feel well, fearless, and stress-free.

Infertility as an unconscious protest

Fertility has been used as a means to oppress women for 3000 years. The Catholic church continues the practice and harms impoverished women in developing countries.

Women have been reduced to their child-bearing function since we can remember. They were supposed to "give" their men many children, especially sons, who they could use as fuel for wars. Giving birth became ambivalent: Mothers knew they would lose sons to war at an early age, and daughters would have to suffer abuse in all imaginable forms.

A woman knows exactly whether her child will enter a good, or a miserable life. Out of consideration for her children she will give birth during a prosperous period, and will consciously or unconsciously enter a birthing strike during bad times.

There are plenty of examples showing this: After the dissolution of the GDR, birthing rates of the new countries halved. The population of the former GDR decreased from 16 to 14 million over 20 years, only a part of which was due to emigration. (Morland 2019)

Similarities to the decline of the Roman Empire are apparent, as well as the downfall of the Mycenean culture in 1200 BC, which saw a dramatic decline of the Greek population for the next 400 years. (Bornemann 1984)

Oppressed indigenous peoples are not only dying off due to genocide, but also because they have stopped having children (Marlo Morgan, 1998, particularly describes this pattern of Australian aborigines).

The Baby Boomers of Germany were not born until 20 years after the end of the war, at a time when the economic miracle ensured high income.

Fertility is highly dependent on psychosocial factors due to the female body's ability to biochemically prevent nidation of fertilized egg cells.

In developed countries like Germany and Austria, women's precarious mental situation is as, if not more, important than their social situation.

150 generations of women were excluded from all rights and development potentialities, being "birthing machines for the patriarchy". The consequences of this injustice are not erased merely by allowing women to work, or the convention of the word-internal capital I. The extensive ancestry of mothers subjected to violence, oppression, and suffering is angrily expressed by the first partly liberated generation of women. It is understandable and undeniable. Nowadays, some men have to pay for mistakes of their fathers and are frightened. It is important to understand the relation, so we, male feminists so to speak, can be patient until the sacred wrath of women subsides. Then we are able to establish a new form of partnership. I have experienced this myself and eagerly recommend it to open minded men.

It is not surprising that emancipated women are hesitant to have children, should they be immediately pushed back into the old schema. I know a young woman whose life was going according to plan: She had a nice partner, they built a house, and the grandparents were longingly waiting for the first grandchild. The pressure was high, and the "ideal daughter-in-law" felt trapped in a golden cage. She broke out and left for a distant city to go to university.

Present-day mothers are in a discouraging situation. Maternity leave impacts their chance of a career, part time jobs lead to poverty in old age, day-care facilities take little consideration of the mother's needs. Mothers without jobs are disparaged as "housewives without purpose", career women are called "uncaring". Who can be surprised that pregnancy may be the last thing women look forward to?

Teenage mothers have been ostracized to an extreme degree until recently. Getting pregnant at 16 would mean rejection, being called a whore. Compare this to native peoples, who would rejoice, for the girl had become a woman. Educated women delay pregnancy as far as possible, to a point when they are told that it is almost too late to conceive a child. But, there are always fertility clinics...

Another interesting detail is the fact that daughters from families with eight, ten, or more children often only have one, or no child of their own. This fuels the suspicion that their mothers did not want that many children themselves, but had no say in the matter. I'm acquainted with the childless daughter of a powerful politician. She has five sisters. After the sixth child, the mother refused to become pregnant again, when all her husband wanted was an "heir". He ended up understanding. Most patriarchs in history did not and insisted on their "marital right".

War of the Roses

Working as a child psychologist, I was often involved in separations, divorces, and child custody cases. Amicable divorces made everything easy, and the children were comfortable with having two separate parental residences, as long as they were able to see both of them.

Many divorces over the past decades escalated in irrational ways and harmed the children in the process. They all showed symptoms of mental strain, from bedwetting, headaches, to behavioral disorders. Fights over visitation rights, alimony, custody battles went on for years. Lawyers did not shy away from allegations of sexual abuse, psychosis, neglect, and so on. These types of divorces are every family court judge's worst nightmare because they drag on for years without an end in sight while sacrificing the children on the divorce battlefield.

Seen from up close, most divorce battles are proxy wars between matriarchy and patriarchy.

Gaining financial independence over the last two generations has enabled women to leave their men, and there is no shortage of reasons to do so. Rigidly patriarchal men lacking understanding for the new rights of women largely find themselves abandoned. Both sides in this situation are spurred on by their lawyers to declare war.

Her: All you've done is smother me, and you never listen.

Him: You refuse to act in your role as wife and mother; you are disloyal.

Without the help of a capable mediator, the situation will escalate and there will be blood. The man insists on his patriarchal rights ("Things have always been this way, I don't know what your problem is"). This outdated rhetoric only contributes to the woman's rising anger. She is tired of hearing such absolute crap.

The true sufferers are the children, whose well-being is only used as a banner of war, not respected. They (almost) invariably want to keep mother and father, and desire more than anything the return of peace.

The sorrow of orphans of divorce will not end until the broad population achieves a new understanding of égalité/equality of man and woman.

Abducted children

All beasts of prey kill the offspring of their rivals, leading the females be ready for conception again. Man has adopted this strategy after entering the status of predator two million years ago. This was not a big problem as long as humans lived in small groups, meaning they did not cross paths often, or avoided others by moving into new territories, eventually populating the entire world.

Agriculture led to a higher population density, and tribes began to fight over fertile land. There was a quick shift to mutually beneficial trade amongst matrifocal cultures. The patriarchy of the last 6000 years forced upon us the predator mentality of the powerful: The lower class was to be kept small enough to discourage revolts. This was best achieved through infanticide and child abduction, an act which paralyzed mothers and decimated the lower class. The Bible documents this practice in two instances: The Egyptian pharaoh killing the children of Israel, and Herod's Massacre of the Innocents (infanticide of jerusalem), which caused Mary and Joseph to flee to Egypt. Infanticide and child abduction carried on as far as the US cavalry killing Native American children, wanting to wipe out the Indian tribes.

Fascist, dictatorial, and totalitarian regimes have brutally abducted and sold countless kids. Human trafficking is still alive and well. Ceausescu of Romania left thousands of children to rot in homes, and used the traumatized shells as his Securitate henchmen. The Balcans were traumatized in similar fashion for 500 years. The Ottoman sultan had a yearly "boy harvest", abducting the strongest boys to train them as bloodthirsty janissary. The fate of Lebensborn survivors in Germany has not been rehabilitated, nobody was recompensed or acknowledges as victims. The worst thing about all this is that predators are continuing their practice unchallenged and unpunished.

Since 1492, children of subjugated colonized peoples had been abducted in order to exterminate the indigenous cultures. Canadian and Australian children were relocated into homes or with white adoptive parents until the 1970s. Catholic children's homes played an increasingly disreputable role. Under the pretext of providing a basic education as well as the right religion for poor, heathen children, the Church alienated them from their parents and traditions.

This practice also survived in Central Europe until 1990. "Trouble kids" were - and still are - taken away from their mothers and put into homes (now euphemistically called "therapeutic shared housing). The conditions present in Catholic homes for difficult children have become public over the last few years: physical and sexual abuse was not an exception, but the rule.

Why are the public authorities - dominated by male lawyers and legislators - refusing to move away from such disastrous practice? Why are they unwilling to help already traumatized mothers and continue to subsequently traumatize them when removing her children?

For years I have had a suspicion that removing children from their mothers is conscious or unconscious intent, which has been gilded as "milieu theory" for the last hundred years. Children start "being difficult" as a result of their cruel (lower class) milieu, so they have to be integrated into a better milieu, meaning a move into state-run facilities.

In reality this is about the weakening and demonization of the "bad" mother. Child abduction is her worst nightmare. It has been perpetrated by the Mafia to defeat and rob their enemies. Why then should state organized removal of children be beneficial?

It isn't. Only in highly specific cases, in which the mother is dead or deeply mentally ill, and social workers fear for the child's life, can it work. In these cases, the best outcome for the child is to be placed with an adoptive or foster mother who loves it like her own.

My experiences over the last 40 years have shown that children of a fragile or sick mother are taken out of the frying pan and tossed into the fire. While they were able to survive on the little motherly connection they had before, they now are left without a mother at all. It is a mystery why they develop into difficult adolescents, despite child services spending big money on homes. It's anyone's guess.

If we were able to explain the womb envy felt by men who take children away from underprivileged and abandoned women through court, make the authorities understand that youth welfare money is more efficiently and effectively allocated in psychotherapie and mother-child therapy, we could help traumatized mothers rediscovered their motherhood.

There need to be mother-child homes instead of children's homes. Experienced women and therapists could help young mothers to discover and manifest their love for their child. "Bad" mothers often had no loving mother themselves, a result of generations of women traumatized by the above mentioned genocides.

If such a mother-child healing were engaged in right after birth, half a year of intensive, stationary help would produce healthy mothers and children. This would also save expensive and useless follow-up costs.

Overweight epidemic

For decades, a global overweight epidemic has been spreading, and medicine has not gotten a handle on it. Doctors' warnings and diets have proven useless. As soon as a population has enough food, about a third ends up being overweight. Significant research budgets have been spent on diets and stomach operations, and every few years a new wonder diet is announced. Participants lose weight at first, but regain their original weight soon after.

The doctors' helplessness is rooted in the fact that they are looking for reasons in the wrong places. Overweight has mental causes. The human body has a ponderostat, a goal weight, which is difficult to change. This ponderostat is unconsciously set to incorporate enough calories in case of catastrophes. The more afraid and traumatized people are, the higher their ponderostat is set by their autonomous nervous system.

Hunger crises are epigenetic over three generations. My own mother was born into hunger in the year 1918. Austria-Hungary and Germany lost the first world war because of hunger crises and the Spanish flu. When a pregnant woman experiences hunger, the epigenetic of a female fetus and its ova is set to combat the dangers of hunger. The egg cell from which I and all my cells grew was consequently prepared for the next unavoidable catastrophe, and dictates a precautionary excess weight.

All catastrophes involving violence of the last 3500 - or 150 generations - have such an effect. Fear of hunger leads people to become stress eaters, and the more fear they have, the more they gain weight.

The fact that we live in abundance nowadays provides little help. Hunger and fear of 150 generations continue to exist in our subconscious.

The overweight epidemic will not cease to exist until the world becomes a more peaceful place, a place nobody has to fear violence and oppression. This means that the violence of the patriarchy is the cause of the excess weight. Getting rid of wars and restoring an egalitarian Man-Woman-Society will solve the problem of excess weight in the process.

A prime example for this is Mexico, which has the largest amount of overweight citizens. The mesoamerican cultures were destroyed exactly 500 years ago, and 90% of the indigenous population vanished. Ever since, a small creole upper class is exploiting the population. The violence of drug conflicts is destabilizing a country which has not been able to recover from the violence inflicted by the Spanish 500 years ago.

Any overweight person can relate: When one feels bad and blue, there's a trip to the fridge to comfort oneself with food.

The oppression of the matrifocal prehistoric society underlines the problem. The ampleness of women is a remembrance of the great Goddess, depicted in countless statues in ample forms. This is a threat to the patriarchy, therefore voluptuous women are degraded as ugly, which is against any sense of reality. (All women are beautiful, Peter Paul Rubens painted gorgeous, curvaceous women.) The retention of weight is therefore a protest against this degradation.

There's more: the desire of a loving Goddess captured men as well. Gabriele Uhlmann (2015) shows that Japanese Sumo wrestlers have to eat until their bodies resemble the female bosom, belly, and vulva imitation. Their fight symbolizes the victory of the patriarchy over the matrifocal Japanese primitive society, going as far as depicting a birthing position with legs far spread apart. The belly of overweight men reminds of pregnant women and is a sign of unconscious womb envy.

V. The cover-up of violence

Genes contradict propaganda

Dictators recognize the significance of propaganda. True power is established in the minds of people. All history books dating until the 20th century were hagiographies of the powerful. They shone a light on the noble acts of kings and emperors. Conquests, killing of rebels and dissidents, as well as victories in battle were thought of as the highpoints of civilization. All nations believe that their citizens are descendants of victorious winners and that rising through the state hierarchy makes oneself a winner.

The truth is different, as genetics currently shows.

Over the last few years, geneticists have been able to trace the migratory movements of humankind based on two genetic markers. A constant rate of mutation of the genetic markers allows us to determine how closely related individual peoples are. Mitochondria DNA (mtDNA) helps us trace the migratory movements of women over the last 200,000 years, while genital DNA (yDNA) allows the same for men over the last 70,000 years.

A wholly surprising image emerges in Europe. Caucasians throughout Europe and western Asia are descendants of various lineages, which were settled across the continent at the end of the last ice age. Although female mtDNA has spread to neighboring regions, the female gene pool as a whole has stayed the same.

The male yDNA comes from fewer lineages, spread across Europe, especially east to west. This is consistent with the conquest of the continent by Indo-Europeans from southern Russia.

This leads to a new image of Europe's population. Genetically, Europeans are 90% non Indo-European, but 99% speak Indo-European languages.

The matrifocal primal population has survived until today, especially in maternal lineages. Basque Genes, for example, are not only found in Basque country, but across northern Spain and southern France as well.

How can this be?

Well, historians assume that Indo-Europeans in all conquered regions constituted a small upper class, the warrior caste, which wielded military power. The native population had to slave for the warriors. This image is true for the Europe of the Middle Ages. 90% of the population was poor and worked for nobles. Knights were living comfortably. Knights (German Ritter from Reiter = rider) were nothing else but an elite military troop of the cavalry (cavalry and cavalier, or chevalier, from French cheval = horse).

Further down the road, investigations will show that especially the nobles have Indo-European genes and are descendants of steppe warriors.

This means that Europe shows similarities to present day Latin America: Only 10% of Latin Americans are descendants of white Spanish and Portuguese. They form the corrupt upper class, which has been exploiting the continent for 500 years. 90% of Latinos are descendants of Natives, black slaves, and mixed races. (People of mixed race had no chance of becoming upper class because they were bastards in the eyes of their white fathers.)

Since the genetic findings of Europe and its colonies are identical, why should Europe's own history be much different? It explains the incestual tradition of the aristocrats. Until 100 years ago, the idea of a nobleman marrying a common woman was out of the question. King Edward VIII of England had to abdicate the throne in 1938, after the impertinence of marrying Wallis Simpson.

Indo-Europeans wanted to keep their martial talents to themselves, creating a pure culture.

Attempts at matrifocal restauration

Any resistance against the warlike patriarchy over the last 6000 years had to be led by men. Women had no chance to succeed and risked being killed. Original female ideas were stolen and falsified.

This does not mean that women were weak or not actively pushing back. They needed support from their weapon wielding men to back up the fight for matrifocal rights. Especially vital for negotiations with the upper class was a male figurehead, due to the unwillingness of kings and earls to speak to a woman.

The matrifocal traditions were pushed to the underground, especially in oppressed classes. The patriarchs did not want to exterminate women, but exploit them. There was little control over what was being discussed in villages and female circles. The "heathen" traditions remained strong, and patriarchal religions were not able to eliminate them. Thus they superimposed their own "right and true" dogmas on the existing pagan ones. The history of the Catholic church is a prime example: The virginal Mother Goddess was changed to Virgin Mary, who conceived Jesus with the Holy Ghost. Ancient Goddesses became Christian saints. In Peru, Pachamama is simultaneously the Virgin Mary and the fertility goddess, so nobody complains about keeping old customs. None of the Catholic dogmas originates with Jesus Christ. They were introduced from 325 to 1870 AD during the ever-smoldering fight against paganism. The dogma of 1870 is proof that the history of the church is laughable, not awe-inspiring. In 1870, the pope lost his Church state and worldly power. In his indignation, he ordered the First Vatican Council to declare him "infallible". This is the reason that nobody is allowed to contradict the pope nowadays. What a way to solve problems!

There have been frequent spiritual rebellions over the last 2500 years, attempts to restore the wisdom of the matrifocal primal society.

The Tao Te Ching originates in the 9th century BC, when the Shang and Zhou dynasties had just introduced the might of the patriarchal empire. The Tao Te Ching is full of matrifocal and mystic wisdom, knowledge which continues to impress today. The patriarchy however did not conceive the possibility of female religious leaders, therefore the Tao Te Ching, written down in the 4th century, was attributed to Laozi ("Old Master"). It is assumed today that Laozi never existed. The Tao Te Ching may only be a compilation of oral tradition, and a way for the Chinese emperor to solidify his authority. Similar concerns about the historical authenticity of "male" founders of religions are raised in the cases of Jesus and Mohammed. It is just as plausible that the protest movements were led by wise women, the narrative then being seized by men and misrepresented in a patriarchal form in their writings. We just don't know for sure what actually happened.

The life and actions of male religious founders cannot be historically proven, therefore only the consequences of religious movements are important for our context. I will not discuss mythological founders, but religious groups.

The most radical protest was dared by the Buddhists. They concluded that power and desire are responsible for worldly suffering (which was a correct analysis of the situation), and reject wars and the killing of animals. Their pacifism endures and has a matrifocal core. This made it easy for Islam to displace Buddhists from India, central Asia, and Indonesia.

Early Christians were pacifists, rejected worldly power and treated women as equals. Most disciples were female, the most important one being Mary Magdalene, until Paul the Apostle degenerated the doctrine. He was a Hellenic apostate, silencer of women. When the power hungry bishops of the 4th century allied with the emperors, the message of peace was cast aside. The bishops incited Christians to murder, manslaughter, and oppression of those of different faith. Only Judaism was not prohibited, since such action would require declaring the Old Testament as invalid. On the bright side, Jews were great scapegoats. (They had killed the Lord Jesus - another falsification. Romans had crucified Jesus the Insurgent, if he ever existed, a common occurrence in the Roman Empire.)

Greek philosophy was a return to observing nature, a self-evident practice for women. What works in nature can be observed and its laws understood. Greeks and Romans build libraries and universities to educate any and everyone, including women. The last principal of the largest ancient university was Hypatia, a female genius, whose calculations of conic sections still apply today. Her intelligence infuriated the Christians to such a degree that it caused them to tear her body into pieces in 415 AD. (Chotjewiez 2002) Consequently, the "merciful Christians" burnt all scrolls, destroyed ancient libraries, and banned all knowledge that did not originate from the Bible. Afterwards, the Catholic domination machinery ran without a hitch and reached a point at which popes tried to ascend to emperors of Europe. All kings would have had to pay tribute. The German emperors defended themselves and were deprived of their power for it. Germany remained a small helpless agglomerate of princes from 1250 to 1871. The papal humiliation of Germany, lasting 600 years and reinforced in the bloody reformation wars, is a primary reason for the two world wars of the 20th century.

The power and decadence of the pope steadily increased to such a degree that around 1500, Pope Alexander VI sent his son Cesare Borgia to devastate all of northern Italy. The conquered principalities were divided among his countless illegitimate children. He casually gave the entire undiscovered world to Spain and Portugal, probably because he was Spanish himself.

This sparked protest by the reformists. They tried to free the common folk from oppression by nobles and bishops. They paid for this sacrilege with millions dead. The invention of the letterpress along with translation of the Bible into German enabled the masses to read it for themselves. It inspired criticism by many clever minds, who were not paid by the church and therefore unbound by its instructions.

Thus proponents of the Enlightenment of the 18th century ended the authority of the patriarchal God, and founded a humanist doctrine of social cohabitation, which led to the implementations of the social state after revolutions in 1789, 1830, 1848, and 1918.

The period of Enlightenment perished, as so many reform movements that came before. It was seized by the powerful, inverted, and reused by the rich. This was the first historically documented case of the patriarchy inverting a grassroots movement for its own use. The social concerns of the Marxists were misused by the Leninists to establish a dictatorship in Russia, eliminate farmers and intelligentsia, and strive for world domination as Russia's new czars.

Lenin's insignificant group of fanatics was paid by German militarists and sent to Russia to destabilize the country. They succeeded and plunged Russia into civil war for four years. Without German money and transportation by German trains, none of it would have been possible.

The militarists' ruse was doubly successful. The war against Russia's czardom was won (until the superiority of the USA forced Germany to surrender), and, more importantly, communism was defamed as the work of the devil. In 1991, the USA announced victory of capitalism over communism, which was in fact not actual communism, but a dictatorship of Soviet nomenclature, initiated by Capitalists. The entire world fell for this sham, and paid for its stupidity with an out of control destruction of the Earth by fanatic neo-liberalists, whose ideological narrow-mindedness equals the Leninists.

The powerful have always been able to end social revolutions by misdirecting the energy of the protesters into the driving force of imperialist wars. The demands of the French revolution were poisoned by the coalition wars to end the revolution and perverted in the Napolean wars. The rebellion against oppression was turned into compulsory military service, using protesters as cannon fodder ever since.

In the 20th century, women took matters into their own hands and were successful. The suffragettes claimed women's voting rights, and Bertha v. Suttner organized the largest peace movement ever seen. It was the second covered up reason for the First World War. In order to stop women's and peace movements, the patriarchs declared an entirely senseless war of the Fatherlands, and drove central Europe's population to the famine of 1918.

The plan backfired. Witness to the deathly silence of 1945 were widows and *Trümmerfrauen* ("rubble women", who helped clear away debris after the war). These women had proven again and again their worth and strength in the factories of war. In 1968, women and young men took to the streets in protest against the Vietnam war. Feminism has been pushing for equal treatment of women in Europe and the USA ever since, and Pakistani Malala and Yazidi Nadia Murad were awarded the Nobel peace prize for their fight against oppression of women. Green movements and NGOs are consistently advocating against the destruction of the planet. For the first time in the history of patriarchy, there is a chance of healing the planet through revaluation of our matrifocal roots.

Spiritual securing of power

According to Harari (2015), humans invented mythology in order to unify larger communities of people 70,000 years ago. Since then we have been able to fantasize about anything not rooted in reality. We can paint images, choreograph dances, and compose music, which challenges our large brain on the one hand, and guarantee unity of tribes on the other. Aside its own language, every tribe has its own mythology about acts of ancestors and gods. These tales are passed on from generation to generation in oral tradition. In this way, every nation creates its own spiritual reality, fostering internal solidarity and external differentiation. It does not matter whether myths follow natural scientific laws. They rarely do, which is why European researchers generally describe the views of natives as primitive and stupid. Those myths and narratives are in fact responsible for providing a common base for diverse people of a tribe. A base in which all can believe. Common belief unites people. They belong to the same tribe, the same nation, or the same religion.

Scientifically, myths are a trick of the brain in order to form increasingly large communities. This eventually leads to national state myths. Our nations are not much different from ant colonies, with clear rules of where to march, and when. Ant trails are based upon chemical communication through smell.

Our brain works in a similar way, by chemical communication of synapses, but is infinitely more complex. This is simplified by linguistic communication of the narrative into stories, which are passed on from grandparents to grandchildren, singers to communities, and experts to nations. The stories evolve and transform from generation to generation. In the best case they reflect the sociobiological environment of the community. In the worst case the people are being convinced of a lie with harmful consequences.

We can infer the myths of antiquity from preserved artifacts. Female statues with all attributes of giving birth - dating from 70,000 to 3,000 BC - suggests that people of the time believed in Mother nature, ecology, the Goddess, and the sacred force of giving birth. Experts back then were female shamans, who assisted women giving birth, had knowledge of herbal medicine, and gave responsible advice during times of crisis. Tribal rituals were about calming conflicts within the tribe. Unity was needed to protect against external dangers. It was essential for the survival of prehistoric man.

Then, civilization was invented, and it was patriarchal. It led Europe's researchers to the erroneous conclusion that human progress is based on patriarchal skills of men.

This is a fallacy.

The patriarchy did not arise suddenly, but developed over a transition period of 5000 years. Matrifocality was in the majority during this period, and all important inventions were made by women or women and men together. The first advanced cultures were matrifocal.

The skills of men were focussed on technology, abstraction, and military strategy. Technology and abstraction rule the world by now, and we are reduced to living in virtual realms. Without the faculties of women, we would have perished long ago.

After achieving military predominance, Indo-European male cultures used their disposition towards abstraction to conquer the world of myths. For 5000 years, they have been talking women and lower classes into the following:

War is the father of all things.

Money rules the world.

The male God requires sacrifices.

Money and Father God are abstractions. Money does not satiate, God has not been seen by anyone, and war is a horrible apparition instilling valid fear in everyone. None of this leads to happiness.

Tangible reality has been the same for 70,000 years: plants grow; mother give birth, nurture and cook; love and nature foster happiness; social solidarity delivers progress.

How did the patriarchy manage to secure spiritual dominion and deceive oppressed people with all this nonsense?

Easy. Chieftains and rulers simply had to replace female shamans with male scholars. Wise women were disempowered, killed, burned alive, and are still devalued as feminist witches.

Male experts have been explaining the world to us for 5000 years. They do not suffer contradiction. They are right, even when they're not. Male legal experts twist the truth, until the rich win any trial. No wonder the word pettifogger is still a thing.

In the Middle Ages, bishops determined what was divine truth or heresy. Punishment for the latter was death. On top of this, bishops were rich sovereigns, meaning their judgment was most likely not very objective.

Nowadays, multinational enterprises and their think-tanks dictate scientific truth. This is good for their profits, especially the pockets of male billionaires. The fact that the planet is being ruined in the process does not interest them.

The Catholic church as an instrument of power and the ideological embellishment of oppression

Many people, especially theological scholars, trace the rise of the West back to Christianity. It is supposed to be morally superior and facilitates progress and technological revolution.

The scholars are right, but not in the way they think. The Catholic church plays an important role in the rise of the West, but not due to mercy, love, or tolerance. The significance of the church lies in its efficiency as a spiritual instrument of power, which played into the hands of the powerful. (I am focussing on the Catholic church because I know its history and rites. Similar sentiments are true for other churches.)

Let's start at the beginning: Leppin (2018) paints a differentiated picture of the first 300 years. "Early Christianity" did not exist. Countless questions concerning various topics were given differing attention by individual groups, discussions which ended up condensed into various gospels around 50 years after Christ's death. Early Christians rejected the emperor's power, but still had to adjust to Roman society. Initially, prophets and wise men set the tone, until gradually the episcopate was established. The conversion of emperor Constantine gave the power-oriented movements an advantage. They allied themselves with the imperial court and designated half of the written religious traditions as forbidden Apocrypha, which only survived in Ethiopia and India. All other religious movements were heretics.

Communion was received in private residents, which at first was nothing out of the ordinary. After all, a communal feast was part of pagan sacrificial rituals. The discussion whether to eat meat and observe Jewish food rituals and Sabbath led to splinter groups. Once the imperial cult was denounced, prosecutions began. New prophets emerged: Marcion of Sinope separated Christianity from Judaism, Mani developed it by adding persian elements. Sunday became the day of the Lord. Constantine named it Sunday, day of Sol Invictus, who was state god before Christianity. Christmas wasn't established until much later, again on the birthday of Sol Invictus. Bishops reserved to themselves the right to baptize, and newly baptized individuals were required to follow authorities. A powerful hierarchy developed, imitating Roman administration since Constantine.

What do we notice? Jesus and his message of peace hasn't been mentioned very often since 313 AD. More than half of the New Testament originates from, or deal with, Paul the Apostle. Paul was a defector who had never met Christ. From 313 until 1950, the Curia in Rome claimed prerogative of interpretation in Europe. If mercy were the motive, we would have never had to endure the dark Middle Ages, nor the cruel colonial modern age.

Why Christmas does not bring peace

The best example of distortion of history is Christmas. It is presented as a celebration of love, but rarely is in practice.

The time before Christmas is very busy for psychologists. Many adults are afraid to celebrate with parents and relatives. Although Christmas is a celebration of love and peace, many families are full of conflict. The hypocrisy of pretending to get along for one day out of the year, when the rest of the year is spent avoiding each other, often ends with arguments and sarcasm. Anyone who experiences this cannot care about Christmas too much. The moral pressure to spend these days at home with one's family-of-origin endures. The desire for peace also remains, but is often unanswered.

I live 5 km from Oberdorf, the birthplace of Silent Night. In late 2018, it celebrated 200 years of the 1818 song. For weeks, police and firefighters dreaded that a flooding of the small town by 7000 tourists could become very dangerous. It felt like an amusement park or an enormous shopping mall.

Why is it so hard for us to find peace and contemplativeness, even when it's drilled into us from every loudspeaker starting in September?

It cannot work. The spread of Christmas started with a lie.

Christmas was devised by two of the most brutal Roman emperors, Aurelian and Constantine the Great.

Aurelian designated December 25th as the birthday of Roman state god Sol Invictus, the invincible sun god who was to help lead Romans to victory in battle.

Constantine the Great declared Christ the divine ally in the Battle of the Milvian Bridge. He made Christians his state accomplices and designated December 25th as the birthday of Jesus, who thereby replaced Sol Invictus as state god and ceased to be a bringer of peace.

For 300 years before Christmas was invented and Christ was made divine, Christians only needed the words of Jesus to spread his message. Christ's birthday was neither known nor important.

Meanwhile even biblical scholars accept these facts, which are mirrored in the New Testament:

Why would we care about historical truth?, the four evangelists must have thought. Matthew and Luke recorded two contradicting Bethlehem stories, John knew that Jesus was born in Nazareth, and Mark did not mention anything about the birthplace, even though (or because?) his gospel is the oldest of them all. Therefore, Christians have been believing in "alternative facts" for 2000 years, being able to choose their narrative from multiple alternatives. Nothing new with Donald Trump. Theologians have no problem with this and solve the problem in a Solomonic way: Jesus was theologically born in Bethlehem, and historically born in Nazareth (Gielen 2019). Imagine an elementary student applying this logic on essays...

Pope Benedict XVI similarly justified the truth about Christ's resurrection. The grave being empty or not is of no importance because Christ's resurrection isn't a biological but an ontological fact. It is true per se, independent of biology, history, and science. What can you say to that much theologic cleverness?

Alternative truths invite many lines of thought: Perhaps the message of peace and love was spread by a woman, and Jesus is only theologically a man in order to better fit with the concept of a Father in Heaven? This would explain why Pope Joan was so threatening to the patriarchs. After she had proven that a woman could lead the church in the 9th century, every newly appointed pope of the Middle Ages had to sit on a papal gynecological chair. The cardinals then assured themselves he wasn't a woman.

Amongst all the skepticism, one famous Christmas miracle is historically documented. On Christmas 1914, soldiers at the western front laid down their weapons. Englishmen, Frenchmen, and Germans sang "Silent Night" together, contributing to the global spread of the song. Afterwards, they continued to kill each other for another four years.

The circle closes: From the birth of Christmas at the Battle of the Milvian Bridge, to Christmas 1914.

Invention of Fake-News

Increased access to education, especially for women, allows us to identify lies more easily. People stopped believing the fairytales of greatness perpetuated by men in power, claiming that only they knew how to run the world. Now the world is dying. However, the biggest fake-news is still sold as divine truth, and critics of the patriarchy are branded as godless extremists for not falling for it. Their skepticism is well founded. It is time to deal with arguments by strong women, who will no longer let themselves be cut short.

How is possible that fake-news has become the larger truth on this planet?

The praised truth starts with, and is based on, the Christian Bible. The Bible remains the most read book on the planet. Fundamentalists in the USA demand a literal observance of its truth and align their politics accordingly. Muslim Salafi are doing the same with the Qur'an and shari'a.

At the same time we know how this truth came about. We are able to demonstrate by looking at the New Testament.

All gospels were recorded 40 to 60 years after Christ's death, so none of the Evangelists were contemporary witnesses. According to Flasch (2015), that amount of time is enough to originate legends, indistinguishable from facts. Contemporary witnesses recorded an original document, telling of the Sermon on the Mount and verbal quotations of Jesus, nothing more. Evangelists copied this original document and embellished it with legends as they thought best. There were at least seven gospels, contradicting each other to such a degree that fathers of the church declared three of them invalid. They were the gospels of Thomas, Mary Magdalene, and Peter. This is especially embarrassing because the gospel of Peter could have provided the true meaning of the Chair of St. Peter. Just to make sure, the original document was destroyed to preclude any stupid questions.

One of the first large Christian communities was established in Egypt, where people had believed in the resurrection of Osiris for 1500 years. Osiris was quickly changed to Christ. According to Pope Benedict, this is an ontological fact, whatever that means. It is similarly plausible that Jesus was only seemingly dead, and was freed from his grave before fleeing to India, where his grave still exists. He may have fled to Kashmir, or eastern Syria. (Fried 2019) None of this would have convinced the Egyptians.

The biggest legendary miracle happened in 313 AD. The persecuted Christians became rulers of the Roman empire in one blow. They destroyed all other European religions and sought to succeed secular emperors under cover of their papal office. Who else could have had their hands in this turn of events, but the mighty patriarchal God of war; the one who, once already, had killed all heathens in the Flood?

Secret Mithraism

Don't get me wrong, this is not a plea for atheism. I believe in the divine universe, reincarnation, spiritual evolution, and the Goddess. I refuse to believe in the garbage sold to us by priestly castes for millenia. Their objective is to better exploit us, and destroy the planet without repercussions. For 2000 years, they have claimed to possess the sole truth and killed millions of people for their pride. This makes the real truth ever more important: For example the fact that the truth of the Church largely does not originate from Jesus:

Christianity and Mithraism were the two most fanatic sects in the Roman empire around 300 AD. Christianity was the religion of the lower class, the cult of Mithra that of the soldiers. The Roman state was in decline during the 3rd century, and emperors were looking for a religious renewal movement to restore courage in Romans. Emperor Aurelian embraced Mithraism in 270 AD, and made it state religion, including its sun god Sol Invictus. Around the turn of the 4th century, Mithraism was more acceptable than Christianity. Diocletian, Galerius, and Licinius dedicated countless temples to Mithra, among others in Carnuntum at the Danube, London, and Paris. Maximian built a mithraeum in Aquileia. When emperor Constantine was battling for power with mostly Mithra-following opponents, he invested in Christianity, since its hierarchy was highly organized. In order to defeat his fellow emperors, Constantine executed an ingenious play: He forced the merger of Christianity and Mithraism to secure secular and sacred power, then sold the resulting religion as a better version of Mithraism. Jesus became Sol Invictus and was worshiped.

This heretical thesis would have had me burned at the stake 250 years ago.

Let us look at the facts: Mithraism was a hierarchical community, whose branches reached across the entire Roman empire. Its spiritual leader was referred to as Pater patrum, priests were called father, and believers called each other brothers. This was long before Christianity used the exact same terminology. Mithraism had seven sacraments, just like the Catholic church. Mithraism included baptism and confirmation, as well as communion of bread and water, or a mix of water and wine. It represented the same as Christian communion, a commemoration of the last meal of the master and his own.

I cannot help but notice more connections between Mithraism and Catholicism than between Catholicism and the message of Jesus. His message died with the destruction of Early Christianity. Catholicism was not very Christian ever since: Bishops incited persecution of Mithraists during the 4th century. Christians plundered mithraea and killed their priests. Overpowering Mithraism only worked because Christians built their churches on the ruins of mithraea. Ancient thought claimed that this practice would cripple or destroy the prior god. Jesus would turn in his grave, if he hadn't left it right after crucifixion.

And pigs can fly!

Weixlbaumer (2017) approaches his topics from the perspective of a lateral thinker, and finds a large amount of contradictions within religions. 10,000 religions fight for every single believer. 34,000 Christian denominations all claim to possess the sole spiritual truth and the singular path back from damnation. Each one of them believes they will absorb all others. Weixlbaumer's unmasking thesis: "All religions have their absurdities", and why should we not be allowed to talk about them?

This is why Weixlbaumer created a faith pyramid, differentiating between justifiable doctrine, local traditions, and unsubstantiated absurdities.

Most people believe in god, and all Christians believe in Jesus. Christ did not know Hell, which was introduced by St. Augustine of Hippo 400 years later. Purgatory arrived 1000 years later, limbus took 1800 years. Early Christians would not recognize present day catechism. The question whether the body of Christ was divine or human split Christianity into four fractions, excommunicating and killing each other after emperor Constantine declared Aryans, Nestorians, and Monophysites to be heretics. Furthermore, Christians fought over iconodulism around 800 AD, until the Byzanthine empress had 100,000 contemnors killed to enable everyone else to continue worshiping sacred statues. Weixlbaumer encourages readers to make their own decisions about faith. Educated people do so nowadays.

Karlheinz Deschner uncovered countless accounts of godlessness in his 10 volume work "Criminal History of Christianity" (Anti-Jewish pogroms, investiture conflicts, the forged Donation of Constantine, cruelty of the crusades, massacre of Jerusalem, murdered Catharists, inquisition, burning of witches, Wendish crusade, Prussian annihilation, burning of Jan Jus, limitless wealth of bishops). His revelations kept me from believing in the dogmas of the church. Like most enlightened people I do not require that kind of paternalism. (Meulemann 2018, Flasch 2015)

Schizophrenia as (schizophrenic due to) chronic denial of reality

Representatives of the Catholic church still think of themselves as moral authorities, tasked with showing their flock their sins. This is astonishing. It may be due to a split perception of reality, leading them to sell a religion of violence as a religion of love.

Let us try to understand, for a moment, the women of the 16th century. They had to watch their most intelligent and respected friends being tortured and burned at the stake by Dominican monks. At the same time, priests were spreading a message of love and turning the other cheek. What an exasperating, schizophrenic message. Victims had two options:

1. Believing the perspective of the perpetrators and renouncing the signals of their own bodies. This creates conflict between id and superego, leading to psychosomatic illnesses.

2. Saying farewell to unbearable reality and drifting off into a fantasy world. This is the brain's strongest shock reaction under intolerable constant pressure or severe abusive trauma. Paranoia, multiple personality, delusions of grandeur, and religious delusions are the most frequent forms of schizophrenia.

Schizophrenia can be traced back to the burning of witches. Accused women would crack under torture, their agonized screams and senseless rambling leading their contemporaries to believe they were possessed by the devil. In reality, fear of death caused them to lose their mind. Some fled into religious delusions, for it was the best chance at clemency from the priestly torturers.

The most famous example of this process is France's national saint, Joan of Arc. Joan developed what psychiatrists would diagnose as religious delusions. She believed she was ordered by God to lead the French army and chase away the English. This played into the French king's hand, even though he likely did not believe in Joan's divine quest. Ultimately, King Charles VII regained his land and Joan was convicted by a French bishop and burned at the stake as a witch.

Careers for women in the Middle Ages were basically being cheerleaders for the troops, and, if everything went well, being burned at the stake. No wonder many women fled into insanity when facing death. Insane women were then dumped in the nearest convent, their lives spared. This process did not spare even the most powerful queens. Joanna the Mad was declared insane and sent to a convent for the reason of intense grieving after her husband had died. She was queen of Spain and Burgundy. Her status did not make a difference. Her son Charles V took her lands and established the empire on which the sun never sets.

Was Joanna of Spain really insane? Historians have avoided answering the question. She was a bitter woman, deprived of power by her male relatives, declared insane and locked up for 46 years as a result of a power struggle.

Anyone would lose their mind in such a situation, locked away in prison, convent, or a closed psychiatric ward.

Since not even the most powerful woman of Europe was able to escape such a fate, simple women were well aware of the danger of the inquisition. Protestants and indigenous American women were left little room to think when the Spanish army invaded Mexico and evangelical Germany.

Schizophrenic patients were deemed a threat to the public and locked away for being unable to separate fantasy from reality until just recently. Nevertheless, the public may rather be a threat to schizophrenics. A clear example is the USSR. During the time of stalinist purges, anybody could be killed, even if they were a staunch communist. People became paranoid, a sign, not of illness, but of healthy assessment of reality. Despite being persecuted, people had to show support for Father Stalin in order to stay alive. This turned reality and fantasy inside out. No wonder people lost their minds or became paranoid amidst the collective distortion of truth. The CPSU even went as far as declaring any resistance against the party a sign of mental illness. Anyone calling out the regime as a dictatorship was sent to a psychiatric ward.

Convents were a common way of neutralizing intelligent and insubordinate women. Hildegard von Bingen was the exception, gaining influence in many fields, like music and medicine. Most nuns were taught to think of themselves as humble servants, and convent school continued to teach this idea to millions of young women.

Ringel (1993) documented the harmful consequences of Catholic indoctrination in the 1980s. I remember having confession class in school. I was a happy child before being taught to fear Hell, the deadly sins, and eternal damnation. I remember many sleepless nights.

Social anxieties have always been a big problem: Young pregnant girls were vilified and stuck in homes, suicide guaranteed damnation, and illegitimate children were deemed second class humans.

Unwed children of priests were impacted especially hard. They had to listen to their fathers fulminate against the sin of unchastity, consciously or unconsciously knowing that they themselves were products of the sins of their fathers without ever being allowed to address the situation. It is a classic double bind, predisposing schizophrenia.

Over the last 30 years, countless scandals involving abuse and corruption were uncovered within the church. They were successfully covered up until 2010 (as in past centuries). When a cover up is not possible, the scandals are dealt with "internally".

Patriarchal counter-reformation in church, politics, and science

Scientific revolutions of the last 500 years have frequently been initiated by Jewish scholars. They were schooled outside Catholic indoctrination, and do not have to believe in ecclesiastical dogmas. Scientists all over Europe soon followed suit, not wanting to be played as fools any longer. The enlightenment of the 18th century freed Europe from the diktat of Catholic dogmatic theology and heralded an era of reason.

The counter-reformation has been busy as well, although the times of "Roma locuta, causa finita" are over. Scientists can no longer be denounced as heretics and burned at the stake.

Or can they?

Have new dogmata crept in?

Modern day patriarchy seems to make concessions. Use of the word God has decreased, and the world is now controlled by ideologies claiming to be the singular truth. Ideologies are irrevocable truths, conceived by a founder or founding community. They cannot be questioned. Read: religions in pseudo-scientific clothes.

National socialist ideology was founded in Aryan supremacy and fate. (Absolute nonsense, for which 50 million people died).

Communist ideology - dictatorship of the proletariat included - was exposed as a dictatorship of the despots. Its claim of just distribution of goods has failed especially miserably. (80 million people had to die for this nonsense).

The capitalist ideology of the invisible hand of the market was left the winner in 1991, supposedly being capable of producing a sufficient amount of goods for all people. As promised, the doctrine is unbeatable concerning production of goods. The big problem lies in "for all people". (Is the entire planet dying for this nonsense?).

Any emerging contradictions and critics are met with an aggravation of the ideology: nationalism found its Hitler, communism had Stalin, and capitalism embraced Milton Friedman.

Don't know who Friedman is? He is the guy responsible for our current globalization mess. He invented the economic doctrine of neoliberalism and the total unleashing of the market without consideration of loss, poverty, or ecological destruction.

The dogmas of neoliberalism infiltrated the central powers of the western world in the form of Reaganomics and Thatcherism. Social democrats under Tony Blair and Gerhard Schröder were blinded, and ruined European social democracy. President Trump is blatantly demasking neoliberalism. First and foremost, it is an efficient tool to enrich the wealthy and dumbing down the masses to make sure they will not catch on and revolt.

People are not dumb by nature, but are manipulated through focussed action by a host of people in powerful positions.

The need to suppress people's intrinsic ability to feel this injustice leads the capitalist elite to fall back on strategies of disinformation, which has been tried, diversified, and perfected over the last 6000 years.

The power elite employ millions of people to perpetuate disinformation: secret agents, lobbyists, bought experts, think tanks, scientists providing proctored studies, lawyers, and politicians ensuring tailored laws to ensure the uninhibited destruction of the planet.

The essential means of disinformation is distortion of truth. It can be identified when a felt truth is turned into its opposite. (Werlhof 2011)

George Orwell introduces "Newspeak" in his novel "1984": oppression is called liberation, censorship is harmonization, criticism becomes conspiracy theory. When 1984 came around, people were glad to see that Orwell was wrong, and democracy had not fallen to dictatorship.

Meanwhile, we have been falling for newspeak for 6000 years, not knowing any better. Orwell's dictatorship has never been a thing of the future, it has always existed.

Looking in from the outside, we can easily identify newspeak. We see Putin try to paint the occupation of Crimea and eastern Ukraine as a justified uprising of locals without Russian involvement. Russians believe this. G. W. Bush used newspeak to talk about democratization of Iraq and neutralizing weapons of mass destruction. We did not realize this until the US destroyed Iraq and opened the door for ISIS. Many Americans still believe Bush's truth.

Fortunately, we have reason and science. Scientists are objective, rational, and avoid dogmas like the plague.

Do they really?

Scientific dogma as a patriarchal instrument of power

Sir Karl Popper, born in Vienna, was the doyen of scientific theory and the originator of critical rationalism, which has been embraced by the global scientific community. They use it to distinguish facts from unproven dogma.

Popper's rationalism is founded on falsification. Truths are not able to be proven, only refuted. A truth is accepted until its opposite is proven.

All knowledge is a body of preliminary assumptions, constantly needing verification through experiments. When an assumption is proven erroneous, the hypothesis, or perhaps the entire theory, is declared invalid, and a new theory has to be developed.

So far so good.

Or not. We live in a world of science but are manipulated nevertheless. It is felt in the declining belief in science and an increase of conspiracy theories. The average citizen approaches facts as potential fake-news, plunging the internet community into a battle of contradictory belief-bubbles.

Critical rationalism works, but only when scientists strictly adhere to it. This is influenced by the fact that, due to neoliberalism, elites own science's funding, opening the door for manipulation and other opportunities.

The simplest consequence is falsification of data or limitation of experiments to non-representative samples.

For example, it is very easy to refute the greenhouse effect by limiting measurements to growing glaciers, omitting all other glaciers from the design. There are thousands of such studies, mostly financed by oil companies.

Scandals involving data manipulation to the point of verifying a desired theory are uncovered every year. The embarrassment is met with remorse, and the sacrificial pawn loses their professorship. Nevertheless, the fabrication pays off, for progress of knowledge has been successfully stalled.

The most important tool of manipulation is the restriction of permissible premises. It is essential in silencing critics, and is frequently overlooked or denied. (The thesis of a harmful patriarchy is not allowed to be tested by principle.)

How does one uphold power over millions of intelligent and educated people?

It's easy.

Every branch of science has assumptions, which are branded as absurd and can destroy scientific careers. Rather than proven truths, premises are only assumption, capable of being tested. When the verification of certain theses is inhibited, possible scientific revolution and the advancement of our conception of the world is stifled.

The following are two examples, which are only seemingly contradictory:

The irrefutable premise of the Middle Ages was the Bible as the source of the singular truth. All science-oriented experiments were regarded devil's deeds and heresy. Most wise women paid with their lives, demonized as witches.

Nowadays it is irrefutable truth that knowledge can only be attained through physical experiments with a material base. Even psychology only accepts statistics which are visibly measured in the human body or brain. All "parasciences" such as homeopathy, astrology, intuition, hands-on healing, or clairvoyance, based on the premise of mental resonance, are excluded from verification. When a crazed, old guy like H. J. Eysenck finds statistical significance in astrology, his studies are ignored.

On the other hand, theoretical physics establishes wild speculations about superstring theory, supersymmetry, multiple universes, dark energy, dark matter, inflation, the big bang, parallel universes, quantum cosmology, and more. All of these concepts have not been empirically tested, because it is impossible. Physics is intoxicated with the beauty of mathematical equations, which have long ago replaced empiricism.

So what's the deal now? Do we have empirical science, or is it a world of speculation?

Well, both: social sciences are choked off by strict empiricism, while natural sciences are allowed to speculate and supply media with incredible headlines.

In reality, experimental verification has led to unexpected, previously undiscovered results in the Middle Ages as well as modern times. Healing salves would have proven significantly effective, and witches would not have been burnt at the stake. Mental effects of parasciences would quickly lead to a holistic worldview, capable of saving the planet.

But saving the planet has sadly never been the agenda of the powerful.

Prejudices of historical science

History is a wonderful science. I have loved it for as long as I can remember, and am carrying on the passion of my mother and my grandfather. I have been reading every historical publication I can get my hands on for the last 55 years, and it has become increasingly more boring. History is rife with mind gag and prohibition of thought. I started to fear I would be wasting my life on proofs, stuck figuring out whether there was an X or a U on a Roman tombstone.

A long life as a psychologist, along with a great amount of clinical knowledge of humans, has led me to understand several theses which would interpret historical data differently than history departments do. Common teachings ascribe the rise of civilization to the Sumerians and Egyptians. Men invented the plow and the wheel, kings established hierarchical administration. The violence of men and the immense physical and psychological harm of war to civilization is brushed aside.

I was saddened to learn that the matriarchy was declared disproven. I discovered the body of work surrounding criticism of patriarchy after being led astray by prevalent publications for years. The thesis of an egalitarian Neolithic culture has since been a logical alternative to popular history, which is preoccupied with victory in battle. I believe in a matrivivial past because it best explains human psychology and their irrational behavior.

Let us compare current literature from a prevalent perspective and patriarchy criticism:

Archaeologist Parzinger (2016) talks about human history prior to the invention of script in his book "Die Kinder des Prometheus" (Children of Prometheus). Starting with the Fertile Crescent, he examines civilizations in Europe, Africa, Asia, Australia and Oceania, as well as the Americas. The expansion of agriculture and sedentariness is depicted as stereotype succession: First gathering of grasses, to occasional cultivation, leading to purposeful cultivation, and ultimately extensive farming and irrigation, ceramics, and livestock farming. Parzinger forgoes speculations and theses. On the whole, he does not introduce anything new.

Dux (2019) presents a complex account of the power struggle between the sexes and how it may have originated, but he does not provide clarification. His core message: In primitive times in Europe, female power over birth and death was more important than any male aspect, and was in fact threatening to men. Examples for this can be seen in present day New Guinea. Their men are terrified of female power and are trying to dominate their women. One must not overlook that there are 60,000 years of separate evolution between paleolithic female statues in Europe and the dark religion of New Guinea. Dux closes with the notion that male power has somehow established itself by fate. There is no insight after reading the book in its entirety.

Uhlmann's "Archäologie and Macht" (Archaeology and power, 2012) shows a bolder thesis. Archaeology and history embrace patriarchal domata, which are akin to prohibition of thought and therefore similar to medieval censorship. This prohibition of interpretation is justified by "scientificity", limiting accepted work to provable claims, meaning only the physical appearance of found artifacts. Uhlmann in turn constructs logical theses: Europe's prehistory was matrifocal and survived without wars. She explains why her arguments are ignored and censored by the commercial publishing market. Acknowledging an advanced, matrifocal civilization would impact and weaken the foundations of patriarchal thinking. In reality, the last 5000 years have been marred by wars and genocides, responsible for human suffering and mental illness in 30% of the human population. I have verified this in my books

"Children of Tantalus" and "Tantalus's World". (Opelt 2002, 2016)

Just as bold is Wunn, professor at the theological sciences institution in Hannover, when it comes to proofs of Christian superiority. The primitivism of prehistoric man has to be established, leading Wunn (2014) to disregard cave paintings and female figurines as proof of a primitive religion. Spread hands and bare female genitalia are interpreted as defensive signals, shielding against danger. She does not explain why Neolithic humans ascribed immense power to the vulva. Female figurines were shielding against the evil eye. Supposedly, primitive man was not able to see past magical explanations (how does she know?). She does not recognize the pillars of Göbekli Tepe as remnants of a temple but claims they are roof pylons of normal houses. All these interpretations paint the picture of a primitive prehistory, setting up Christianity as a beneficial force. Wunn never tries to deal with the idea of the great Mother, the center of Neolithic religious conscience. What about spread legs and the vulva as symbols of birth and creation?

Wunn doubles down on her tendentious view in "Barbaren, Geister, Gotteskrieger" (Barbarians, Spirits, Divine warriors). She tries to establish a scientific voice by claiming all interpretations of paleolithic traditions to be false. She wants to prove that characteristics of evolution (diffluence, mutation, selection) can be found in religious movements. Religions adapt to their social and biological surrounding and its changes, meaning religions are a product of their biosocial environment. This does not get along well with divine inspiration. The book's scientific approach is both its strength and weakness. On the one hand, Wunn debunks religions of the book: There existed neither the empire of Solomon nor Moses' exodus from Egypt. Both were written legends dating around 700 to 500 BC. On the other hand, Wunn reduces the neolithic period to descriptions of surviving artifacts without examining ideas and conceptions of the times. To reduce images of birthing women to protective magic is to brand prehistoric man as primitive. Such claims are not supported by archaeological data.

Böttcher (2000) delivers a great example of male dogmatism. He sees the origin of Indo-Europeans among the Funnel Beaker culture of Central Europe, which emerged when "vikings" tried to dominate the Ertebölle culture of Central European Linear Pottery. In the process of Indo-European germanizing, upper classes of Indo-Europeans and lower classes of native peoples were established. The viking ship as a weapon of conquest has long been replaced within scientific discussion with the Kurgan chariot. Böttcher's book shows how subsequent conditions are projected onto the neolithic. The belief that Germans were the original Indo-Europeans, held by national socialists, has long been proven false.

While professors have been abusing their authority to defend antiquated theses, new theories have been kept away from faculties. It is true that pre-astronautics, civilizations sunk into the ocean, and old, highly advanced technologies are unproven, but they are hypotheses which should be treated and examined as are supposed blessings of the patriarchy. It would be embarrassing, should such "speculations" turn out to be true.

VI. Healing of fear and anger

Fear and duress/compulsion

Animals utilize fear as a survival mechanism to escape predators. The first predator, Anomalocaris, was hunting trilobites 500 million years ago. Ever since, all animals have developed an alarm system, reacting to threats with three actions: when the predator is recognized, the animal feints death in order to be overlooked. An approaching predator triggers the escape reflex. If escape is not an option, the animal will attack the predator and defend itself. Any dog owner knows this succession when observing his dog approaching a rabbit. The rabbit ducks before running away. If he is caught, he starts dealing blows and can easily defend himself against individual house dogs.

Prehistoric men acted similarly, having the additional option of climbing a tree. The amygdala controls the reaction process. The body is flooded with adrenaline to achieve maximum performance. If escape was a success, the adrenaline will be depleted within a few seconds. Prehistoric humans were rarely stressed longer than 15 minutes because that is how our system is built.

Modern man is more complicated. The amygdala directs any signs of threat over the hippocampus into the cerebrum. Any human experiences thousands of stimuli capable of raising alarm in connection to their life story. Even worse when the origin cannot be accurately identified. The cerebrum will then identify and remember many unspecific signals as a threat. People with trauma or a troubled youth are constantly chased by fear reflexes. The body will pour out cortisol to manage continuous stress. Cortisol in turn will at length damage organs, making people sick.

Anxiety disorders are the most common mental disease, taking various forms: panic attacks, phobias, obsessive-compulsive disorders, depression and psychosomatic dysfunction, and so on.

These symptoms can be traced back to anxiety reflexes of animals:

Flight: One tries to escape and avoid danger. People with phobias panic when stuck in a dangerous situation, therefore avoid planes, elevators, mountains, and speaking in public.

Freeze: All movement is ceased until danger passes by. Depressives stop leaving their beds or houses and cease all activities.

Fight: People with compulsions are desperately trying to regain control over the situation, often with repeated stereotypical rituals. Fearing a fire breaking out in their home, a person might double check every flammable thing 100 times, which can take up most of his free time.

Continuous stress due to extreme or persistent traumatizing: Body functions are impaired by increased cortisol and organs are damaged in the long run.

Fears and compulsions are normal to a certain magnitude to ensure survival. A healthy person learns how to deal with danger and overcome their fears. Avalanche risk is a good example. Most people sensibly avoid entering such slopes, and extreme skiers practice and develop their skill and danger assessment to such a degree that they could ski down Mt. Everest unharmed.

There are two extremes:

The extremely courageous who overestimate their abilities. They tend to die quickly.

The extremely fearful who break out in sweat when thinking about a standard, secure slope.

Anxiety disorders are treated by a moderate amount of danger training. Approaching the frightful situation in small steps can help to control one's fear over time.

Panic attacks and depression are especially hard to treat because the patient has no clue what they are afraid of. They are afraid of everything, because everything can lead to a panic attack. Long term psychotherapy can help discern unconscious sources of anxiety, they are often found in the persons childhood or family history. Depth psychology can be especially helpful. One quick method to find hidden sources of anxiety are professionally led family constellations led by a clinically experiences psychologists, psychotherapist, or psychiatrist.

A person suffering long term from anxiety and compulsion should contact a professional and seek help.

Causes of psychological illness

Doctors and psychologists from different fields have been fighting about the cause of mental illness for 100 years. Should not any sensible person be able to conquer their fears?

The military toughens up their recruits so they can endure extreme danger and are willing to risk their lives. Many GIs return from war zones either traumatized or in a casket, and a large amount of survivors struggling with psychological illness cannot cope with social networks and can end up homeless. Psychotraumatology has researched and verified that war efforts and violent experiences are a significant trigger for anxiety disorders.

Trauma research is a new field, soldiers and victims of violence were left alone with their fears until recently for a simple reason: if the victims' suffering were acknowledged and taken seriously, fighting wars would quickly be a thing of the past. Which sensible man or woman would voluntarily be killed as cannon fodder?

As seen in the first part of this book, most men of the last 6000 years would. What had rotted their brains to the point of running toward death with their eyes open?

There had to have been a significant amount of brainwash. Men are not stupid and suicidal by nature (some cynics would disagree). They must have been told many beautiful things about death.

We know the key words: Fame, honor, immortality, a perfect life beyond, 77 virgins for every warrior, ultimate victory, battle for justice, Fatherland, nation, religion, ideology.

All these terms are intangible: We can't touch them, see them, or buy anything with them. They are all things located outside reality. Critical young people of the last 50 years hit the nail on the head: All bullshit! In other terms, these are political or religious ideologies invented by some man for a specific purpose. It is usually the same: Ideologies exist to make young men stupid and suicidal in order to give old men money, power, and reputation. This trick ensures and perpetuates patriarchal power.

The glorious promises are carrots in front of mules, making them blind to the precipice they are being led to. The tricks change with time and trend. Now, it is God's will, next the nation, then the promise of conquered land, money, wealth. Men have been dying for their nation – what ever the epithet – for 200 years, before then nobody even knew what a nation was. The Spanish died for silver and gold, the crusaders for the pope and his power, the Marxists for Stalin's dictatorship. The reason essentially does not matter, as long as the dead meat follows the standard-bearer.

Secret agencies and powers in the background know that the central goal is to confuse both enemies and their own sacrificial people. Disinformation is spread not only by the KGB and CIA but by all think tanks throughout time, ever since the patriarchy was established. The Fake News of Trump, Putin, Erdogan, Madura, and others has never been anything different.

The most important means of gaining power through war and violence is the cover-up of violence and its victims. Violence cover-up has been successfully anchored in our brains for a long time, and we have stopped scrutinizing it.

Even so, contradictions of disinformation are easy to see:

Why should Jesus – who chose crucifixion over taking up arms – demand of his followers to take up the sword and storm his thousands of years old grave? It would be a ludicrous idea nowadays, but that is exactly what Pope Urban II told his crusaders, sparking a lasting conflict between Occident and Orient.

Germans followed Hitler for people and Fatherland, until the Fatherland was destroyed.

Communists died for Stalin, who imprisoned survivors in gulags.

Hitler consoled himself with his victory over the Jew, before blowing his brains out. He indeed expelled Jewish critical intelligence from universities and lastingly replaced it with party line loyal people who glorified violence. Similarly, Stalin killed Russian intelligence as Mao did with the Chinese.

All these situations delayed people's self-awareness for 100 years. In the early 20th century, Depth psychology discovered that renunciation does not solve consequences of violence and abuse, they continue to exist in the subconscious and make people sick. This knowledge is still seen as suspect in psychological research, although it has already revolutionized the world view three generations ago.

Strictly speaking, most of the brain is now home to unconscious, repressed things. This state is in turn denied and nothing allowed to resurface.

Patriarchosis

Patriarchy critics give consequences of 6000 years old warlike patriarchy the name patriarchosis: It is a collective illness, denying causes of violence which endure in peoples' souls and lead to more suffering and violence. Nations are indoctrinated to, while experiencing suffering, not acknowledge it through collective rationalization. We are being fed false premises which are branded true by God, by science, by industry, by the financial elite.

We are successfully convinced to work and consume ourselves to death, for the planet to progress to death.

We are told that humans have no soul, and science is therefore only allowed to examine individual nerve cells. Any wasted thought concerning our human nature is unscientific humbug. People interested in our soul are forced into the underground, and are branded as a laughable esoteric movement.

We are trained to eat a lot of meat, along with one billion Chinese. The Amazon jungle is cut, the soy harvested there is then transported 10,000 km to Europe where its fed to tortured animals. The animals are slaughtered as soon as possible, their meat transported 10,000 km to China, so its population can eat as unhealthily as we do. It is obviously idiotic. The main priority is of course company profits and making millionaires.

Something is seriously wrong here.

Awareness of war victims' suffering

The awareness of war victims' suffering developed in the mid 19th century (Goltermann 2016). Until the Napoleonic wars, death on the battlefield was a natural occurrence, a stroke of fate, and a consequence of personal guilt before God. Only victors and heroes were remembered, victims were culpable for their own downfall. Even Tolstoy's "War and Peace" only criticizes Napoleon's arrogance, not the war itself.

The Crimean war of 1956 saw the first treatment of wounded based on medical knowledge (Florence Nightingale). It followed statistical capture of war casualties and medical epidemiology. The military wanted to minimize casualties to optimize their expense factor. Bacteriology charged commanders with responsibility for hygiene, ensuring soldiers' survival. Victims were therefore only seen as such after identifying persons in charge of minimizing "losses".

Attempts to civilize war and limit its worst damages started in 1864. Rules were established accordingly in the Haager conventions of 1899 and 1907. War gas and especially harmful ammunition was later also outlawed. Only, nobody followed rules in war. The Propaganda war started, an effort to put the enemy in a bad position by accusing them of wartime atrocities. International law during war established itself against partisan war. Franc-tireurs were excluded from the Geneva convention and were treated miserably. The oppressed had to defend themselves against asymmetrical warfare of the powerful.

Victimology was developed after 1945, with PTSD being discovered in 1980. World war veterans afflicted by "war jitters" were at first dismissed as pension neurotics. Only after NGOs helped spread victim attribution in media, showing the alarming state of affairs, the general human populace has started to become aware of the magnitude of consequences of war.

Anger and aggression

All animal will defend itself in the face of danger without escape. Even a small field mouse will bite a human's hand when caught. Musk oxes chase away polar bears by females forming a circle around the young, and males attacking with their sharp horns. Male testosterone ensures survival.

Prehistoric man was no different. The larger and more muscular men formed an outer ring of defense while women formed the inner ring, collectively protecting their children. Aggression was a means of self-defense and survival.

After the invention of the spear, men were on the offense and killed rivals before they could become threatening. Soon enough they started harvesting meat and became hunters.

The patriarchy utilized the male offensive force to oppress women and start new wars to accumulate power. This has been reinterpreted as defensive instinct for 6000 years. The supposed enemy was first to attack, oneself had to defend oneself to protect women and children. As late as 1975, conscientious objectors (draft resisters) were baited into portraying themselves as liars by being asked: "Would you take up your weapon if the enemy threatened to kill your wife?" An honorable man had to respond with "yes" and was promptly whisked away to war.

As long as wars have existed, men have been trained to be soldiers and to kill efficiently. They are taught to endure wounds and mortal danger by ridding themselves of their emotions. Losing their fear of death and inhibition to kill is called "high troop moral". Is killing highly moral? This inversion of morals by the military has worked for a long time, and still does in the US and war movies.

It is no surprise that men have a hard time of embracing peaceful behavior after returning from war. Generations of men were taught the killing trade and were defined by military victories.

War shows the schizoid division of social evaluation of aggression. Violence against enemies is highly moral, whereas violence against one's own countrymen will lead to the electric chair. During times of partisan war, the definition of good and evil can change at a moment's notice. Combatants are gambling whether they will finish with a noose or a medal around their necks.

Even worse when the ideological valuation system is reduced to absurdity by reality. Many Vietnam veterans went to war to defend freedom, only to despair when finding themselves caught in a neoimperialistic conquest, a daily massacre of Vietnamese civilians.

Children who are raised with such contradicting double messages risk becoming schizophrenic. Is it surprising that traumatized men become violent, beating their women and children, ending up terrorists and running amok?

People born in the 1950s were caught in outbursts of violence by surviving Wehrmacht soldiers, prone to violent trauma flashbacks under stress. We were alert to being beaten and screamed at for no apparent reason. The average father did not cross a line, but extreme aggressive behavior was readily absorbed by their sons.

Violence inspired aggressive behavior and personality disorders among men spread across countries around the world, and the weak suffered for it. Women, children, and gentle men paid for violent wars. "Strong" men with personality disorders are insufferable to their wives and pay for it with relationship problems, divorces, and separation.

There may come a point when one feels anger in oneself, an anger which does not relate to any current occasion and will not subdue. This anger originates from unprocessed violent experiences of our fathers and male ancestors. All my male ancestors throughout generations have been affected by war and military, and their heritage of anger has not been satisfied. The Middle East and Africa are ravaged by violence. This epidemic of violence has to be stopped to avoid being flooded by asocial psychopathies.

Healing the violence epidemic

Humanity has survived plague and cholera and exterminated dangerous microbes. The worst epidemic poisoning our brains is overlooked by scientists, denied by politicians, and justified as God given by priests.

This epidemic harms the souls of perpetrators and victims, the former becoming brutal and numb, the latter frightful and helpless. Wars, genocides against humans and animals, rape, expropriation, displacement and oppression are its many forms, the downfall of humankind and the planet.

Contradictory to common doctrine, war is neither God given nor inextricably linked to our genes. The war epidemic is 6000 years old, only one second of our 5 million years of human history.

Healing is not only possible, but easy and cathartic once the problem is acknowledged.

The cover-up of violence and genocides has to stop. Wars should be ostracized, the perpetrator-victim cycle need to end in the heart of humans and nations. Perpetrators have to apologize to forgiving victims for all to find peace. This works very well in family constellations and genocide constellations, even descendants of Nazi culprits and gassed Jews can reconcile. This can only work if injustice is admitted and expressed. As long as injustice is denied, the anger of the oppressed can not fade.

Jewish genocide coping strategy

The Jewish people had to suffer and survive 2600 years of violence and genocide. They are the oldest surviving culture alongside Chinese culture. While China – in its mountainous seclusion – has been a mostly unified country for 2200 years, the opposite befell Judaism. Located amid the old advanced cultures of Egypt, Anatolia, and Mesopotamia, it has remained a perpetual theater of war. No wonder it was the birthplace of a monotheistic religion of God, the Father, protecting His people against all enemies. No other nation had to suffer from patriarchal excesses of violence as the Jews had. All others in similar situations did not survive.

Tradition dates the beginning of Jewish suffering to the yoke in Egypt and the Exodus. The oppression of the last 2600 years is historically documented. There have been three short periods of Jewish autonomy since 750 BC: The first from 750 BC, when king Joshua made monotheism the state religion, until Babylonian exile (600 BC). Next, 100 years from the Maccabean revolution to the conquest by Romans, and finally the Israeli state since 1948.

How does a nation survive, one that has endured constant oppression, banishment, massacre, thousands of years of pogroms and genocides; a nation which has been demonized and made the scapegoat by the powerful wanting to justify the next genocide; a nation whose suffering was only acknowledged after 6 million humans, a third of the Jewish population, died in the Holocaust?

To survive the great collective despair, Jews developed a tradition of "survival regardless". It involves solidarity, old rituals of dance and humor, and especially the continuous handing down of tradition by scholars, rabbis, and bar-mizba communities, in which all adult men were able to participate and discuss. Killing their people did not touch the Jewish spiritual and cultural knowledge. They did not relinquish interpretative primacy over their fate to their oppressors. Genocide was recorded as a genocide, massacre a massacre, expulsion an expulsion. No bishop was able to twist their fate and portray the expulsion from Spain in 1492, or the expulsion from Germany, as a divine act of God.

Saint Cyril of Alexandria, the church father of orthodoxy, violently destroyed the largest Jewish community of the time. He incited angry Christians to wreck the library of Alexandria and dismember Hypatia, principal of the largest ancient university. What a healthy dose of sanctity! Judaism was the only ancient people to record this.

I hope Jewish scholars will forgive me for simplifying many issues. I am trying to underline an important point: Jews were the first people of the world to develop resilience against violence by perpetuating truth and unmasking lies. Cover-ups and suppression lead to stupidity and illness as shown by Jewish Sigmund Freud. Truth and discussion of truth nurture intelligence, likely the reason why Jews are the best educated people on Earth. The world is not a disk underneath a crystal dome, a belief perpetuated by the Catholic dogmatic until modern times. There are many worlds, all of them round, and perhaps inhabited by intelligent beings – Giordano Bruno was burnt at the stake for that statement, at the Piazza del Fiori in Rome, by order of the Pope. That things are much more complicated than we have ever been able to imagine was proven by Jewish Albert Einstein.

Holding onto an acknowledged truth is what has been changing the world in spite of murders and massacres.

Judaism is the first successful resistance against the violent patriarchy, and it is persecuted and hated for it. A fallback to the matrifocal system aids survival: Any child born to a Jewish mother is Jewish itself, even if conceived through rape by an enemy trying to eradicate the Jews. Matrilinear acts are the answer to dictatorial hate.

Democracy

Europe credits itself with the development of democracy, the most modern political system and the victor over the dark Middle Ages. Democracies are an efficient means to control dictatorial systems. This does not mean that patriarchal exercise of power is not present in democracies.

According to patriarchal historiography democracy was founded in Greece. That is how we learned and believed it in school, though it does not stand the test of reality.

Democratic votes were only held in Athens, a city founded by

Pelasgians, the matrifocal native population of Greece. There may have existed some remembrance of voting within an egalitarian native population around 500 BC, resurfacing after the expulsion of Athenian tyrants.

Only free Athenians, a minority, were able to participate at the agora, and even they were controlled by a few oligarchs who could have unwanted rivals exiled or killed. Socrates was one of those forced to die. Women, slaves, and men not born in Athens had no voting right whatsoever. Dictators around the world would salivate over an Athenian voting system in modern times. This hypocracy dissolved quickly after Athens ascended to the top, oppresses all other cities, and lost the Peloponnese war. After Alexander the Great, all Western nations were founded on strong autocrats, portrayed as "good kings", who demanded absolute loyalty from their cannon fodder. This lasted until 1688 AD.

Democracy was invented by the British during the "Glorious Revolution" under Dutchman William of Orange and his Scottish wife Mary. The British and the English had been a collection of despots and conquerors from all over Europe (Saxony, Danes, Norse, French) for 1000 years. The English nobles had killed each other in the War of Roses, the throne taken by a Scotsman, Stuart. The people had had enough of constant oppression. Sadly, the first English revolution was discredited by Oliver Cromwell, a worse tyrant than all kings before him. In 1688 however, the British chased away the final Stuarts before reaching out to William and Mary. They achieved a constitution which gave parliament a say. This led to many small steps towards limiting the king's power, until Queen Elizabeth II is only able to read speeches written by the prime minister.

As with all rebellions the British was an attempt to reinstate egalitarian principles of a matrifocal native population. Usually, rebellions are crushed and the insurgents put to death. The Glorious Revolution of 1688 was the first to be bloodless and succeed, perhaps due to Britain being the last European country conquered by the patriarchy (Celts in 300 BC). The Island Celts kept matrifocal elements, such as druids, village communities, a right to redemption instead of punishment, song as remedy, tree and plant culture. It is a beautiful aspect of Irish culture, or what English colonial rulers have left of it.

Precursors of democracy in Scotland, Switzerland, and Holland were helpful in the process. The Swiss cast out the Habsburg family, Scots beat the English, and the Dutch trumped Spain, the mightiest nation of the time. The transition from Scotsman Jakob Stuart to Dutchman William of Orange made a constitutional monarchy possible.

Democracy was further developed in the American constitution of 1787. It leaned on the six tribes of the Iroquois, a matrifocal culture on the road to an Indian nation, until the murdering white colonists entered the picture.

The French revolution of 1789 was inspired by the American constitution, and therefore by the Iroquois, giving a new meaning to the punk mohawk of the 1980s. Democracy in the rest of Europe is about 70 years old. For 150 years the patriarchy employed any means necessary to fight against loss of power, leading to Europe's devastation during the Napoleonic wars and the two World wars. The principles of the American constitution were only accepted in Western Europe once everything was ash and ruin in 1945.

Our democratic lime-wash is thin yet. Dictatorships in Spain, Portugal, and Greece endured for a long while. Right wing populists, dreaming of old patriarchal times, are on the rise. This is partly because US democracy is in a crisis, having yet to process the extermination of native Indians and enslavement of black people, paired with a puritanically veiled blindness of thinking God is on their side. The neocolonial US empire was built on war, exploitation, and double standards. Economical exploitation by billionaires is even more efficient than military exploitation. The phrase "America first" has been law for 200 years, and Trump is the court jester blurting out the truth.

There is much still to do to establish an egalitarian and respectful society which does not destroy Mother Earth.

Truth and Reconciliation Commissions

Nelson Mandela is a 20th century hero. Like Bertha v. Suttner, Gandhi, and Martin Luther King Jr, he has proven that liberation of humankind is better achieved through peaceful means than violent ones.

He establish the Truth and Reconciliation Commissions to process decade long suffering of apartheid. White and black, perpetrator and victim had to sit together, discuss, and agree on what is truth and what had really happened in the past. Nobody was allowed to take the other's truth from them, differing truths were able to exist side by side. Right and enlightenment were the goal, not revenge and punishment. This blossomed under Mandela's presidency, cover-ups vanished, South Africa remained peaceful, and white people were allowed to stay.

It was a new way, better than past revenge, a new majority beating down a new minority. Everyone was invited to talk, everyone was being listened to, everyone was taken serious. Communication replaced revenge.

Sure, South Africa has a long way ahead, there are relapses of corruption and kleptocracy. The truth commissions were a good start to helping the country move away from terror and destruction.

In order to overcome the collective trauma of a country, truth has to come to light. Its fate can be processed once the lies end. This is how it works in psychotherapy as well as on a national level, proven by South Africa.

But what has far off Africa to do with us?

A lot!

All countries, peoples, and nations need truth commissions to overcome the shadow of their past. Germany has gone through such a process, evolving from a fascist to a peaceful nation. Lying about its cruel past is illegal there.

Simon Wiesenthal demanded right, not revenge. He tracked down perpetrators of the Holocaust and was branded a hostile for it in Austria. Most people wanted to forget the past after the war, but that does not work. Aryanized goods had to be returned, murder had to be uncovered, or murder will never stop.

Most countries of the world have yet to start the search for truth. Genocides have to be called by name no matter which ideology justifies them. As an Austrian, I know how liberating it is to apologize for the faults of one's ancestors. When I was a child I believed in the kindness of my mother – as all children did. I believed her justifications ("Of course we were Nazis, everyone was in the party"), never asking why. So it is ever more important to look, grieve, kneel, and ask victims for forgiveness. If truth can be spoken, it is possible to liberate oneself from the weight of the past.

Many truth commissions are needed, for the losers and especially for the winners.

The US needs a truth commission to discuss the crimes against native Americans and slaves, to apologize, and to practice rituals of peace.

Catholicism needs a truth commission to discuss the crimes of the inquisitions, forced conversions, and abuse offenders, to acknowledge and atone. The world needs more than a non-committal lip service without consequences.

England needs a truth commission to discuss the crimes of colonial conquest and exploitation around the globe, to apologize and vow betterment. The pride and arrogance of the self-opinionated will never end otherwise, and they are in the process of steering England into a brick wall.

Every country of Latin America needs a truth commission to discuss the murder of Indians, the exploitation of mestizos, and the theft of land in order for the continent to recover.

Australia, China, India, Russia, Turkey, they all need truth commissions. The world needs truth.

Truth commissions are especially needed to discuss the historical and current violence against women. These commissions need to be 50% women, representing the female victims of the patriarchy.

Only then will we recognize that genocides, violence, and torture are not a good way to the future.

Collective trauma therapy

All of humankind has been poisoned by the patriarchal violence epidemic over the last 5000 years. Pain, anger, and fear have seeped into the collective subconscious of every country, every town, every region. (Gasperl 2018) Anything suppressed does not disappear but haunts our dreams and is reflected in our fears for the future. Sensitive, emphatic, and thin skinned people will get sick because of it.

Holistic medicine tries to cleanse the body of waste and negative energy. Doctors cut open abscesses, remove cancerous tumors, and bacterial plaque. Humans in psychotherapy cleanse their souls from fears and aggression. All of these fields are working to cast off the negative and the exhausted.

Everyone can start the purification with themselves and by doing so get healthier. The sick and suffering are doing themselves a service by seeking help in individual psychotherapy. Family constellation help to understand one's own history and the traumas of one's family. Personality reinforcement through self-awareness is more efficient for problem and illness prophylaxis than any medical intervention.

Even better is liberation through rituals withing the community. Truth has to be spoken and affirmed. Differing views have to be endured until a tolerant consensus is reached. Remembrance celebrations at memorials for victims unify the participants and give them strength for a new beginning.

A real dialogue between men and women instead of pseudo-equality is urgently needed. Both sides have to listen to and respect each other, recognizing one another's values. This will take a long time, but will make a return to an egalitarian native society possible. A society with a common purpose to save the Earth. Men will initially struggle to imagine forfeiting their old privileges, which have built them a comfortable nest. Men pay for this privilege with frustrated female partners, leaving them at one point or another. Men have much to gain, but it takes listening and learning. Caring for newborns and toddlers can heal the emotions and open the hearts of fathers. I carried my daughter in her first year as much as my wife did, got up every second night if needed. It was the happiest time of my life, for I have never felt so much closeness and love.

Once us men are able to overcome being afraid of our partners due to unconscious guilt over past injustices and start acknowledging them as competent training partners in life, we will quickly discover a deepening of our emotional abilities. Psychosocial skills will be essential for future professional development, so it would be to the men's benefit to listen to women's suggestions. This may well be the recipe to soften resistance. With a little practice we will be able to establish a whole new life of joy, love, praise, and pleasure. Our partners can teach us how to heal our maternal wounds inflicted by the patriarchy.

Social learning

Children are our future. This phrase has deeper meaning than empty speeches suggest. Our relationship to our children is the best chance to put our past behind us and create a new and evolved future.

We recognize our inner wounded child in the feelings of our children. Parents and kids change their life together with every game, every laugh, and every joy experienced. Being present with our children, we remedy old deficits and fulfill our wishes. Someone who used to be lonely as a child will experience as much closeness as needed as a father/mother. Someone who was oppressed will become as free as a bird. Someone who was abused will define healthy boundaries of peace and security.

This is the mothers' wisdom, experiencing the enormous power of life during the fetus' growth, the newborn's birth, and the development of the child. The divine power of the Goddess would nourish women and men alike. Men would experience this power while caring for their children, leading and accompanying them through life, together with their women. Men grow peaceful and kind when they feel safe, close, and loved. The warring patriarchy destroyed the feeling of closeness and opened the original wound of man. Do some children really like to kill their pets and torture animals? Most kids are naturally vegetarian until told that their body needs animal protein, which is untrue. We can all be loving and loved men, women, and children, as long as we do not abuse trust, disappoint, or abandon each other. Children living in security are a treasure we must protect.

The image of growth seen in nature has dramatic consequences for the education of our children. Our present school system is a crusty relic from times of absolutistic kings aiming to breed obedient underlings. Children follow a certain curriculum to be eligible for certain jobs. This is perpetuation of old guild order, its main goal being the exclusion of competitors (not sure why a bad grade in math would exclude someone from creative, medical, or language studies). Pure knowledge transfer is harmful nowadays, impairing the brain's flexibility. When certain knowledge is acquired, it is already outdated. It is useless to teach children handwriting they will never use, the 10 finger system on a keyboard is significantly more important. Sadly, impressively educated experts are still typing using the two finger search-and-destroy method, never having learned simple and significant techniques. We have to encourage our children to realize that they can teach themselves and how to gather readily available information. Instead of staying focused on their weaknesses – which children are naturally uncomfortable to deal with – we need to encourage them to spend time and energy on their biggest interests and strengths. They will teach themselves more than a lesson plan could.

The school of the future is a psychosocial-creative workshop with plenty of opportunities to experiment. Empathy, communication, and creativity are basic techniques just like reading and writing used to be. Old cognitive techniques have long been replaced by computers. We should make use of it as a base to enable every human being to develop their own unique place within our world, to be successful and happy.

When we elevate respect and exuberance, feeling respected and loved, our errors will cease to be a measure of worth and turn into opportunities of betterment.

The organismic feeling of one's own body is a measure of life. All abstract images and perspectives have to be aligned with one's intuition to avoid being harmful and counterproductive. Carl Rogers recognized that a division of cognitive views and physical feeling can make a person sick. Freud noticed the same with a ruthless superego oppressing the natural wishes of the id. Cultural views oppressing life need to be replaced.

Mothers are close to life, and their feelings are not emotional babbling but the rhythm of life. Men do well to trust women's intuition.

VII. Social balance

A lot will change

I do not, as a man, have the right to explain birth and female emotions to women. They know best. The works of patriarchy critics (Gimbutas, Armbruster, Bott, Uhlmann, Wolf, Werlhof) have described the particulars of an egalitarian society where female perspective flows into the common thought process, redefining the foundation of civilization. Communication and cooperation are essential.

This book is a plea to listen to wise women. The following describes the baselines of a society in balance with itself and nature:

1. Men had their chance. Male thought has brought us technical progress and prosperity no one wants to give up. Blindness towards nature and the wish for peace has plunged our world into dangerous imbalance. We need to stop acting one-dimensional, adopt a new systemic-ecological way of thinking, and slow down technological change. This way we can estimate consequences of change based on existing empirical data before taking new steps. Bitter experiences with innovation has led medicine to a long-winded approval procedure for medication, angering the pharmaceutical industry. Technology has not gone through experiences like the Contergan scandal and is therefore unchecked. 20 years after implementing new technologies we experience negative consequences. Global destruction of the environment is the consequence of blind belief in progress. As every new technology was instantly marketed, recognition of nature's destruction has been delayed for 30 years and is arduously corrected at best. It is an inefficient, irresponsible, short-sighted, and harmful way to act. Mistakes of the past are neither discussed nor are appropriate steps taken. There are many examples: River regulations of the 19th century were a huge financial burden at the time, and billions more are now spent to restore them. Dismantling nuclear power plants costs more money than has ever

been earned with nuclear power. A similar situation is fluorochlorohydrocarbon, which at least showed that the self-inflicted ozone hole can be repaired. A current example is the destruction of the oceans by the plastic industry. The uncontrolled internet-ization leads to addictive behavior, surveillance, espionage, and crime. We are warned about genetic engineering. Damage caused by untested manipulation of human genes and birth process will lead to a psychosocial catastrophe. We need to replace our view of "carry on" to "think ahead", extending past daily politics.

2. A balance of man and woman on all layers is needed, from homemaking to caretaking, jobs, life opportunities, to theoretical structures. Being afraid of each other is a consequence of historical patriarchal violence and leads us nowhere.

3. There needs to be a balance of social classes, peoples, and human and biological life forms. The Indo-European patriarchal upper class must not be allowed to continue exploiting the majority of humans and bio-systems, thinking it is their earned right. People need to know in their heads and hearts that every human has equal worth. Woman, man, homosexual, heterosexual, urban, rural, hunter, gatherer – every human has a right to fair opportunities, their own chosen lifestyle, and the appropriate means.

> 4. There needs to be a balance of humankind and nature in which humankind integrates into ecology instead of destroying it.

> 5. Childbirth and life, instead of death and destruction, have to be at the top of our value system. Taking has to be balanced with giving, every life has to be respected. War and violence are to be shunned. An international police force should be responsible for the security of all humans, living creatures, and ecosystems.

The upcoming paradigm shift

Our present is similar to the end of the late Middle Ages. Theologians had created a closed school and proved the unwavering truth of the Bible through arguments of scholasticism, rhetoric, logic, and philosophy. Then followed natural science and discounted everything humankind believed in.

Authorities used all means necessary to defend themselves against this change. Giordano Bruno was burnt at the stake after foreseeing cosmology and exobiology. Galileo Galilei saved his own life by denouncing his "false doctrine". Charles Darwin was laughed at, called a "monkey", by creationists then and now. Nonetheless, the Theologians' authority is a thing of the past.

Physics has taken the place of theology and has plunged into wild speculations concerning the universe, which are as unproven as 500 year old church dogmas. Logic was replaced by mathematics, and scientists are desperately trying to calculate theorems existing only in their own minds.

A satirical comedian put it this way: Checking the fridge for leftover beer makes you a scientist. Claiming there is leftover beer in the fridge without checking makes you a theologian.

One might add another sentence: Claiming there is leftover beer in a fridge existing in a parallel universe makes you a cosmologist.

Theoretical physics has been treading water for 40 years after leaving the area of observable facts. Ludwig Fleck (1980) calls this the terminal stage of a theory, fated to be scrapped.

European science has been revolutionizing our world view for 1000 years, employing logic and mathematics of the left hemisphere. They are male strengths based on linear If-Then strategies and at their most efficient when trying to pick off prey or reach a set goal.

This way of thinking does an injustice to a hyper-complex, globally connected world. Ever larger computers are needed to deal with immensely increasing data. This gives rise to the fear that a central supercomputer and artificial intelligence will rule and exploit us. Strange, in science fiction movies the superpower is always portrayed as a woman. Amazon's "Alexa" follows this pattern.

Humankind will survive if it recognizes its fallacies. Fear of a global hyper-intelligence is nothing else than an old patriarchal fear of Mother Earth's revenge against its wayward children.

Humankind's fear is subconscious remorse about the patriarchal oppression of women and ridicule of female thought.

Female thinking has always been connected, originating from a need for overview of the whole while raising their children. Women are better at intuitively registering connections in their entirety. Female intuition, often vilified, is nothing else than beneficial use of, and trust in, nature's largest computer, the human brain. Our nervous system, consisting of 300 million cells and trillions of synapses, will beat any technology available when it comes to an assessment of the human condition. The so-called gut feeling, originating from all nerve and body cells, trumps any rational decision. The human body is the largest measurement tool evolution has ever produced, and women know how to read it.

Instead of fearing supercomputers or the end of the world, it would be more meaningful to correct the ruling imbalance. Female intelligence will help us to reconcile with Mother Earth. The integrated approach of women will radically change our world view like Copernicus' discovery of the heliocentric planetary system did 500 years ago.

The answer lies in the ocean

We are looking for answers 13.8 million light years into the distance. While the Big Bang will never be observable, we need not look further than the tip of our nose: the bottom of the ocean.

Our ancestors were aware of the Water Goddess, the strongest form of the Great Goddess and protector of life, death, and reincarnation.

Nevertheless, we treat the ocean horribly, the origin of life and 70% of our body (The ocean's salinity is reflected in our bodily fluid and essential to the function of our nervous system).

We treat the ocean as if it were our biggest enemy; over-fishing, poisoning it with chemicals, oil, and plastics, destroying life.

Depth psychology recognizes the ocean as a symbol for the unconscious and the intrauterine world of the fetus in the womb. The unconscious is full of treasures to recover for humankind to advance to its full potential.

Ignoring our oceanic and womb origin will unbalance the world. Our continuing destructive streak points to a subconscious complex, an error in our psychological system. We are convulsively sustaining this complex to avoid confronting a painful realization.

We are slowly coming to this essential realization. Once the ocean dies, Earth and humankind will follow. Without ecological change we will not survive.

The central premise of our thinking is enduring: Our logical (male) thought with all its technological inventions leads to progress and prosperity.

Well, yes and no.

Male thought, being in control for 6000 years, has achieved as much progress as possible with help of technology: nourishment, energy, goods. We have reached a level we would not want to live without.

What has not been achieved so far are peace, luck, harmony, and social justice. For that, it takes the wisdom of women.

What do women have to do with the ocean though?

World history retold

We are now becoming aware of our lacking knowledge of Earth's largest area. The deep sea, at 4000 meters, is an unknown planet barely about to be explored.

Our global climate is controlled by ocean currents. The increasing weather extremes in Europe depend on Pacific waters flowing east or west near the equator. Ocean temperature controls desert growth and monsoons. Arctic ocean temperature is responsible for the slowing of jet streams and consequential alternating droughts and floods in Europe.

Empires of the last 5000 years did not fall do to lacking leadership but sudden climate deterioration and droughts. Not even supreme courage in battle helped.

Augustus, Charles the Great, and Genghis Khan had luck with the weather. They founded their empires during warm periods. Fog, wind, and rain were decisive for victory in battle. For example, the Spanish armada lost to a storm, not the English. Storms prohibited the rescue of the West Roman empire and Mongolia's conquest of Japan.

Nevertheless, humankind has experienced breathtaking development from primitivism to ever increasing progress over the last 5000 years. Or so we are led to believe by historiography, anything else is ignored.

Students are still being taught that the Sumerians were the first civilization. Unfortunately, the pillars of Göbleki Tepe (27 circular structures with 270 pillars, weighing 20 tons each!) contradict that claim. 12,000 years ago, neolithic man displayed a level of masonry not reached again until the Egyptian temples 7000 years later.

This fact is quickly explained away. Göbekli Tepe was humankind's first building, the remaining – and immaculate – stones somehow deposited by hunters and gatherers. Historians are wildly calculating how a few small tribes were able to exhibit workmanship not seen again until an Egyptian work force of one million people. Archaeologists, to avoid unearthing more contradictions to their theories, stop planning further excavations after uncovering 1.5% of the site. (Like judging Vienna based on the Favoriten district).

What if Göbekli Tepe is just the only structure of the times we have found by chance?

There are so many indications for this, one really has to shut one's eyes tightly to not see it.

All nations on all continents has myths involving sunken cultures. The biblical flood can still be true. The Hopis of Arizona know of five universal floods, and Atlantis has been on peoples' minds since Plato.

But those are just fairytales with rational origins, right? The Atlantis myth has its roots in the volcanic eruption of Santorini in 1627 BC, or the flooding of the Black Sea in 6700 BC.

Scientists make sure to draw correct conclusions only when the subject is supposedly too far away to concern us. The history of Australian aborigines, for example, is quasi taboo for historians. They are aware of the important evidence of aboriginal culture buried under the sea. Sea levels were 120 meters lower when aborigines conquered the continent by ship (sic!) 50,000 years ago, staying level for 40,000 years. Humans commonly settle near the water. The old aboriginal settlements are all together sunk under the ocean.

Feels almost as if Australia were on another planet. We know the specifics of European coastlines during the first ice age, but who would think about looking for cultural evidence underwater there? Those myths are all fairytales anyway, right?

We are aware of a sudden hundred meter rise in sea level of the Black Sea in 6700 BC. Even so, nobody has searched it for lost cities. When Haarmann (2013) suggested doing so, he was told to keep his linguist nose out of archaeologists' business.

Maritime archaeology has existed for 30 years. Its scope has been limited to known concepts, like the palace of Cleopatra and sunken ships. It's a start.

Reports of cyclopean masonry and roads have amassed with an increasing interest in deep sea diving. Amateurish accounts are ignored, lacking professional credentials (Too bad archaeology was founded by amateur Heinrich Schliemann). Historians have better things to research, something about the house of Habsburg maybe, or some bullets from World War I.

Civilization will soon expand to the shelf sea to build oil rigs, wind parks, and aqua farms. The amount of enthusiastic divers will increase as well.

The laws for inhabiting the sea will closer resemble land law in 20 years. A maritime archaeological salvage excavation will have to be conducted before any concrete can be poured. This will lead to discoveries able to turn historiography on its head. The warring patriarchy will become a footnote in world history: a crisis-infused transition from neolithic ecological balance to global balance of an ecological human civilization.

The list of lost lands yet to be explored is long: the Java Sea and Malay Sea, the East and South Chinese Sea, the Sea of Okhotsk, the Red Sea, Persian Gulf, Gulf of Gabés, the Aegean Sea, Adriatic Sea, Black Sea, the English channel, the Gulf of Mexico, the Bahama Sea, the waters of New England and Newfoundland, the mouth of the Amazon, the ocean around Argentina, the sea between Australia and New Guinea – all of these are shelf regions which used to be above sea level 12,000 years ago, the time of Göbekli Tepe's grandiose masons. Atlantis and Lemuria can be lost ten times over in these lost coasts. Is silt and sand really all there is to be found? Educated professionals seem to think so without ever looking.

The mercy of retirement will soon save professors from having to justify themselves for their outmoded views.

Gender-feminism as equalization on a patriarchal base

Will women and radicals ever be satisfied? Our standard of living is as high as never before but still there is only criticism. Feminism has liberated women and brought them to power. What else do they want?

Sure, feminism has achieved preliminary equality of women in western society, enabling them to go to university and have careers. An increasing amount of child daycare facilities allow them to combine studies and careers with raising children. Other continents are just starting the emancipation process and will match our progress at length. Eliminating the pay gap and glass ceiling to achieve legal and financial equality will take some time, although we already see women in leadership positions at large companies. For the first time ever, German chancellorship is passed on from one woman to the next.

The focus of equality so far is an insistence on women being equal to men. Women are supposed to be free to do anything a man can, including a military career. The ideology backing this way of thinking says that there is no difference between men and women, meaning all sex differences are acquired. Gender feminism leads to a unisex phenomenon, with women wearing the same jeans and coats as men. Dresses will be an exception worn for balls and weddings, menstruation is made invisible through technological means. Being a mother will be a concealed minor matter, not to get in the way of one's career. Political correctness will hijack the conversation and admissible word endings will take the spotlight from actual important topics.

The patriarchy is quietly moving towards another victory. Mental and economic foundations of patriarchal society are unchallenged and untouched. The powerful will graciously grant equality to women, turning them into better men, requiring acceptance of male theory. Career women will have to deeper internalize male discipline and rationality to compete with male colleagues, and children are often cut out of life planning in order to not fall behind.

The total victory of patriarchal capitalism will be a consequence of emancipated women insisting on patriarchal rights. Full time working women doubles capitalist potential for exploitation without anyone noticing. A larger work force also leads to increased production and higher environmental impact. Karl Marx knew that a large army of deployable workers serves employers, allowing them to decrease wages and abolish employee rights. This pattern can be observed over the last 20 years. Precarious working conditions without social rights are increasing, newly industrializing countries are employing millions of women in low wage jobs, forced to unpaid overtime and kept like slaves. Women burn to death in textile factories without safety measures. They are baited with emancipation, being told they would earn their own money, before being stuck in sex work and low wage industry. Millions of women work in wealthy patriarchal countries while their children have to grow up motherless at home.

It might be easy for Europeans to avert their eyes from exploitation in foreign countries, but it makes them blind to exploitation in their own homeland. The insistence on full time work for women, uncritically adopted by labor unions, leads to self-exploitation of European women. The keyword double taxation hides a health catastrophe already present in the burnout epidemic. While men were 100% breadwinner and women 100% homemaker about 100 years ago, nowadays both men and women are almost 100% breadwinner. This means that almost nothing is left of the 100% family management handled by women about 100 years ago. Either women have to work 200%, or children come up short. Even if men were to split their responsibilities 50-50, which rarely works, both men and women will have too much on their plate, leading to burnout.

"Successful" emancipation with a fair half-half split in a patriarchal environment will plunge underpaid families into existential crisis. Both parents will burn out long before reaching retirement age, and lose their ability to work and income.

The trap springs. The overpriced rental apartment in the city and everyday expenses require two incomes. Accumulating savings is generally impossible with a exploitative banking system, low interest rates, and high taxes. Losing one income will drop the family into the lower class. Losing both salaries leads to a permanent struggle with minimum collateral. Single mothers lead a life at the precipice of poverty.

Sham emancipation is a new move by the powerful to keep women small. Women are facing a challenge which will lead to feelings of guilt in any outcome. Either they earn too little and are neither equal nor adequate, or they are missing time with their children and are branded as bad mothers. The lack of child care, a result of economic pressure, is a burden on day-care centers and compulsory school pedagogues, who complain about immature, badly behaved, and badly raised children (state organized help with child care has not yet reached a sufficient level, lacking after-school supervision and adequate day-care opening hours). Mothers will always draw the short straw.

Megatrend women

Women are not stopping half way: futurologist Matthias Horx (2014) acknowledged and calculated the importance of women for the development of humankind. The period of peace since 1950 has seen a steady continual rise of education and significance of women. This trend is statistically independent of all daily actualities and political moves, and has global weight: All countries with access to education and work for women experience an increase in influence, general prosperity, cooperation, and willingness for peace. Extrapolating the steady rise since 1950 into the future, the "female" peace and ecological movement will reach an influential majority in the year 2070.

Influence and activities of women have been changing the world for decades. There has never been as much prosperity, knowledge, and opportunities for this many people. People are slowly realizing that the world might not perish after all. Steven Pinker (2018) uses statistics of the last 100 years to show a continuous improvement of all measures of global society. People are getting wealthier, older, more educated, and healthier. Child mortality, diseases, war, and murders are decreasing. Global average prosperity is now the same as 1950s United States. Even though the environmental problem has not been solved, global society is meeting the issues head on. Our culture has improved raw materials efficiency. Small phones can handle dozens of functions for which we used to need many instruments, LP records, and whole libraries.

Pinker attributes the enormous progress of the last 200 years to the enlightenment period with its protagonists Smith, Kant, and Hume. Reason and natural sciences have steadily gained influence since then. Faith, myths, and religions have been replaced with nature observation by modern man. Progress is based on examination instead of ideology. Reverse conclusion shows the rise of women made possible by the disempowerment of patriarchal religion.

Women's impact is bigger than men's in many areas – medicine, psychology, and pedagogy are largely carried by women. Health related occupations are experiencing a paradigm shift from rationality to intuition, energetics, naturopathy, and holistic medicine. Even gynecology is slowly returning into women's hands.

Women are leading economic progress in developing countries, i.e. Africa and Asia. They generate revenues and manage money. Grameen Bank only grants micro-credits to women, guaranteeing efficient use and repayment. Many women furthermore practice traditional gardening, feeding their families as they did in the Neolithic period.

Female power is inhibited by patriarchal and corrupt-cleptocratic structures in many countries. Powerful men are defending themselves by paying low or no wages for women's jobs. With increasing access to education and resistance against antiquated prejudices, the days of the patriarchs are numbered. Feminist sciences are developing opposite poles to old dogmas. The oppressed base of society recognizes lies and is defending against them outside of outdated established power structures. Men and women are uniting in NGOs, 15 years old students are driving global economic forums to and fro to such a degree that they believe their only way out is to shoot the student. Nevertheless, strong women like Malala and Murad survive in order to expose men at the UN plenary meeting.

The wind of change is blowing and will not be stopped.

Egalitarian matrivivial future

The world will find its way back to an egalitarian society over the course of the century. Matrivivial knowledge will regain its value and return to being the foundation of cohabitation. All our ways of thinking we believe to be essential to our society will become obsolete.

Mothers value all children equally. The Goddess values all beings equally. Constitutions include equality, but the powerful are using any trick they can to trod on it.

Money and power will cease to erroneously be put on a pedestal. Power does not lead to happiness and money cannot nourish. Work and service will soon be defined differently than today. (Bregman 2017)

Only one who works should receive financial earnings – one who is gifted money will get lazy – such is common belief. Scientific experiments prove the opposite: 13 homeless were given money to fulfill their most important needs. 9 of them were able to recover and leave behind homelessness. Decades ago in one Canadian and four US cities, people were given an unconditional base income. All of them experienced an increased standard of living as a result, citizens using the money to renovate apartments and establish businesses. People would work approximately 9% less than the average worker but were more efficient and enthusiastic. Sickness and social costs decreased to the point of saving the state as much money as they spent on base income. These results echo insights of motivation psychology: People work at their best when motivated. Things we like doing the most, we do the best, since we spend our time practicing them. Bregman uses this recognition as the base of his utopia. What if 10 million people could be their most authentic self without existential worry? There is no question that everyone would find their most fitting occupation and excel at it through intrinsic motivation – wanting to be proud of oneself. If extreme athletes can motivate themselves to participate in an Ironman (26 mi marathon + 1.9 mi swim + 111.4 mi bicycling), we can be sure that many people are capable of extraordinary performances. The creative output of humankind would exponentiate if no one had to struggle with existential fear while doing undesirable work which machines will soon replace.

The powerful are still trying to control us by instilling fear. A closer look shows that the rumored dangers are not real and their arguments ridiculous.

Existential dread is incited by counting off all the jobs soon to be replaced by machines. Even respected scientists like Yuval Harari are contributing to the fearmongering, erroneously argumenting like cheap tabloid journalist. Technological disruption is supposed to be one of the biggest dangers to our civilization (Harari 2018), as if history professors don't know that every past technological innovation created more jobs than it replaced. We should be glad to get rid of senseless, stereotype labor, leaving more room for interesting and creative work.

It would be great if artificial intelligence were to replace all technological jobs! We would have time to work on all the things the patriarchy ignored and left underserved. Human work has been shifting to more intelligent occupations over the last 500 years. In the beginning there were hunters and gatherers, followed by farmers and cattle breeders, then came craftsman and merchants, industrial workers and businessmen, service providers and scientists. Soon all of us will be social and creative workers. This opens up the opportunity for a global society to return to a higher standard in matrivivial community. The knowledge of mothers will be of central importance.

The sanctity of birth

Life, not death, was holy until 6000 years ago. It was represented by sacred birth, the vulva was the threshold to life and reincarnation. The Goddess was the loving mother of all life, nature was a paradise giving people everything they needed. Even the Bible describes paradise as the Garden of Eden, a peaceful, nourishing place for humans and animals.

Paradise is a garden sustaining life, not fostering murder. Return to such a place, wanted for millennia, is possible if we sanctify life again.

Valuing the wonder of birth has to be part of it as well. People are not only physically born in the perinatal period, their luck, self-awareness, and ability to love is impressed. Newborns need to experience love to develop stability and mental health. Contempt for pregnancy and childbirth as female necessities without meaning are a collective patriarchal lunacy inducing depression and schizophrenia. Once we can stop serving machines we can focus on nourishing the mother child connection, creating aptitude, personality, and stability with every minute spent with our kids. Caretaking will soon be the most important occupation, and teachers will be smarter and wiser after being educated in all emotional disciplines. Money will be spent on sustaining happy mothers, father, and kids instead of weapons to kill them. Love, connection, and care obviate social and mental illness. Instead, the patriarchy is spending billions on pathogenic circumstances and treating the people after they get sick. For every well-adjusted, well supported mother, one fewer psychiatrist or psychologist is needed. What do psychiatrists do?

They treat early stage disorders and their consequences with biochemical means – an expensive, inefficient, and futile system. A psychotic whose illness stems from absent motherly love won't be cured by antipsychotics. Young mothers need to be supported financially, emotionally, psychologically, nourishing motherhood and the connection of mother and child. "Bad mothers" are, in reality, abused and unhappy mothers in a deficient state of patriarchy built on disrespect for the feminine.

Investments in commitment and relationship

Humans are clinging and social beings. Their primary needs are to be carried by their mothers after being born and held by the community after learning to walk. We need connections, bonds, and relationships to feel secure and overcome fears. Humans have been forming communities of up to 150 individuals for millions of years, growing strong enough to overcome all obstacles. They traversed straits and high seas 70,000 years ago, adapting to extreme climate conditions. They were successful by sticking together.

A person cannot survive their first year of life, not being able to walk, without a mother. Being carried establishes a primal bond, primal feeling of safety, and life assurance, connected with body heat and love. In nature, baby monkeys which fell from their tree have a miserable chance of survival. Similarly, orphans without mothers have a low chance at a successful life. There is nothing worse than being all alone.

Let us draw a conclusion. The suffering of the past must not have been in vain. We have achieved the material base of prosperity able to support a return to emotional commitment and the happiness it creates. Any person on their deathbed realizes this, wishing for more time and closeness to their loved one (not money or power).

Power is pseudo safety for the patriarchy, unable to replace real feeling of security. The most powerful men were tortured by paranoid fear of being hated and consequently assassinated. Millions had to die for Joseph Stalin's paranoia. Power brings unhappiness for subjects as well as the rulers, who often end up being murdered, like Gaddafi, or committing suicide, like Hitler.

Mothers know the road to a paradise of emotional joy. Love, life, and nature is everything a being needs. Liedloff (2017) discovered this years ago: Amazon Indians who lack commodities but are supported for a long time are happier than us wealthy adepts of civilization. Let women show us how to nourish and grow our "gentle" souls. It will improve happiness more than any fortune, fairytale castle, or expensive trip around the world.

There is enough for everyone: equilibrium economy

The economy has been growing exponentially for 200 years. We are producing enough food and goods for 10 billion people living in prosperity. Hunger and poverty of the last 5000 years have been a result of a small upper class exploiting the majority and a disproportionate allocation of goods.

Equilibrium economy was common around the globe until 3000 BC. Small tribes and communities shared everything in order to survive. Everyone had to be well fed to stand a chance against predators and natural disasters. Most primitive peoples still lack the concept of property. Agriculture is practiced on common land. Everyone takes part in working the field and is supplied by the community with anything they need. This explains why native Americans had no concept of buying or losing land by putting three Xs on a scrap of paper. The Shona and Matabele people of Rhodesia (modern Zimbabwe) and the Kikuyu of Kenya were robbed of their lands in 1890, taken by the English with the reasoning that the lands were rightfully ownerless and therefore belonged to white people.

Behavioral biologists assume that our sense of community, not our weapons, saved humankind from extinction. Mutual support led to healthy hunters and gatherers, living almost as long as present day Europeans.

Hunger, poverty, and epidemics originated with the owning of property. Indo-European nomads accumulated herds of cattle, and for the first time the powerful owned more cattle than the weak. It got worse with every country conquered by Indo-European leaders. They established themselves as an aristocratic upper class and exploited indigenous populations. There has been rich and poor ever since. (Epidemics first arose from close contact to farm animals.

Landed gentry ascended to money nobility during the industrialization and has since been exploiting the majority through capitalist means. Wealthy people desperately craving for recognition is the only logical explanation. Who needs three castles and 20 cars for anything but to show off?

A human being cannot eat more than 2000 to 3000 kcal per day without gaining weight and inviting sickness. The nobles of the Middle Ages paid for their excessive consumption of expensive meat with painful bouts of gout.

The return to equilibrium economy can be easily accomplished. Fully developed concepts for it exist, but are blocked by the wealthy spending millions to prevent the end of their power.

1. Social market economy

John Meinhard Keynes, F. D. Roosevelt, and Ludwig Ehrhard established an integration of the masses into the economic circuit, securing widespread prosperity in Europe and the US from 1932 to 1979. High wages, state transfer payments, and high savings interest rates encouraged consumer spending and economic growth became a self-seller. Unfortunately, Neoliberals canceled out the social market economy after 1980. Since then 50% of global wealth has been in the hands of the wealthiest 1%. They spend it on useless commodities such as luxury yachts, unused vacation homes, and destructive prestige projects like nuclear power plants, rockets, and gigantic dams in the jungle. This leads to apparent (but bogus) growth and unproductive capital destabilizing financial markets as well as destruction of capital in stock market crises, after profits were skimmed by the rich of course. This intensifies poverty and housing shortages. Wealthy Englishmen and Germans are buying inner city property in Austria for short weekend trips while Salzburg, Innsbruck, and Vienna residents cannot afford a rental apartment. (Schulmeister 2018)

2. Public interest economy

Christian Felbers' (2010) concept puts a hard upper limit on wealth. Anyone can accumulate wealth to the point of being able to fulfill all their dreams. Large unused wealth without purpose is prevented by the upper limit and distributed to common welfare in forms of charitable donations, investments, millionaires' tax, or research, education, and health sponsorship. There is enough money to ensure a carefree life for all citizens. The reward for public spirit is a social one. Donors and helpers will be loved and happy.

3. Unconditional base income

Every citizen receives a national base income to cover basic needs and prevent existential worry. This helps many people who are either recuperating or cannot work due to illness. Others might want to continue their education. The majority will soon become bored doing nothing and will spend their time on self-actualization. (Maslow 1973)

It is claimed that these conditions are not financially feasible, which is false and purposefully misleading. GDP distribution is inefficient and money does not find its way to the ones who need it, due to chaotic bureaucracy, corruption, arbitrary grants, and crony capitalism. Ideologies lead to a significant portion of money to be spent – without effect – on a social security "hammock", promotion of fossil fuels, ecological destruction, luxury pensions for the few, and generally being wasted on "high culture" for the rich. Accordingly, daily breaking scandals are exposing the anti-social doings of the rich.

In fact a third of the population is enjoying an unconditional base income while two thirds are driven to a health-endangering existential battle.

The largest group of income recipients while unemployed are retirees. I have been enjoying the privilege for a year myself and can only recommend it. I do not work less than before but experience fewer worries and more joy in life, spending time on the things I like doing and know how to do best. I am sick less often, saving hospital costs and delivering higher quality work. Every healthy retiree finds an activity with purpose. Mine is the spread of expert knowledge through writing books and holding seminars (the traditional task of elders of all cultures). Many grandparents carry out unpaid and priceless care work for their grandchildren. Education systems would have collapsed long ago if it weren't for grandparents' commitment. Others take on honorary appointments which would not exist without unpaid volunteers. The redistribution of pensions system will soon be at an end, being unjust and not financially feasible. It has to be replaced with an improved system: an unconditional base income.

Even the sick and people fit for limited employment are currently receiving an unconditional income at any point in life, though they have to navigate the humiliating machinery of bureaucracy for it. All social, labor, and health authorities would become superfluous if citizens did not have to constantly explain oneself for unpaid periods in their life.

The highest income while unemployed is paid to rich heirs and stock owners. Some are lazy and their character rots. Others, despite having financial security, strive for responsible occupations and become leaders in politics and economy.

If the redistributed GDP (40%) were divided evenly by the number of citizens, everyone could enjoy a padded base income. It would even be cheaper than the current redistribution chaos of intransparency, injustice, bureaucratic blockades, bad planning, and misallocation of money for publicly unwanted projects. Personal responsibility of citizens would increase after they take more control over their own life. A just distribution would furthermore create a real market economy focused on peoples' needs instead of serving the rich few.

4. Combination of meaningful measures

Prosperity, contentment, and health would rapidly increase through a combination of all these measures. A secure base income prevents existential dread, inner denunciation, burnout, and deterioration. It increases motivation, personal responsibility, and self-determination. A democratically negotiated upper limit will close the income gap to a generally accepted proportion of 1 to 10. Between these limits, every citizen is free to choose their life trajectory.

The objection that the economy cannot function with an income gap of 1 to 10 is erroneous. Business founders are already investing all their money to build up their businesses, creating economic growth. This should be encouraged and improved. The gap of 1 to 10 only applies to private income for one's own consumption, all larger earnings have to be put towards productive investments and donations, or they go to the state. This process will lead to above average earners investing in crowdfunding projects and businesses. A true market economy for infrastructure and investments will be born, directing funds into directions favored by the majority. Ecological, social, and cultural investment will have the same opportunities presently enjoyed by technological investment. The economy will be democratized when voting and direct democracy is conducted via bank account and block chain. State taxation of many sectors of society will be needless. Speculative banking systems, excessive bureaucracies, and enormous state apparatuses will be superfluous. If, for instance, the police performs their job well, money raised through crowdfunding can pay more salaries than taxes. When corrupt US police shoots defenseless African Americans, their salaries will vanish in a flash. Priests who abuse their altar boys will be permanently unemployed. Company executives who lie about emission numbers or environmental damages can kiss their bonuses goodbye, instead having to give up down payment. Military personnel will lack funding – public as well as secretive – for dangerous weapon technologies, developed under the pretense of "state security".

The rich problem will vanish. As with any self-employed person, turnover will be split into thirds; private income, redistributive taxation, and overheads. The wealthy will be allowed to privately use their inherited or surreptitiously obtained money on a 1:10 income limit. Their millions will have to be invested in projects of use to society. Earnings from selling companies or stock will have to be reinvested in community projects. This will regulate production of useless luxury commodities. The wealthy will have their happiness forced upon them. They will be happier as popular and respected patrons and sponsors, using their millions to gain immaterial value.

The market economy will not be suspended by these combined measures, but rather be truly established without interference of power monopolies and financial oligopolies.

Ultimately the biggest grievance of our present society would be easily solved. The biggest injustice of our current civilization is the worthlessness of care work for child-rearing and support of the weak. Both is still put on women's shoulders and secures their discrimination. In the future, mothers (and eventually fathers) would receive an unconditional base income as payment and appreciation for raising our children. Support and health of children would automatically increase, and mothers would be able to earn additional income based on age and needs of her children. The poverty trap of low pensions after being home taking care of children will be replaced with the base income.

Our true needs

We strive for fake needs under the patriarchy. The pursuit of money and power does not make one happy, but addicted. According to Maslow (1973), humankind needs four needs fulfilled to lead a happy life:

1. coverage of nourishment, living, and lifestyle

2. need for security

3. the desire for social acceptance

4. self-actualization

All our needs are covered by one person at the beginning of our lives. The mother nourishes, protects, and loves her child. Under her protection, the child can flower.

Similar duties were fulfilled by the Neolithic tribe. Life in and with nature nourished, the group provided safety and social acceptance, and everyone was able to be their true self within the community. Primitive peoples are happy as long as they are left alone. Catastrophes are challenging but can be overcome as a unified tribe. Life amongst native Americans was so attractive some white people started to live as Indians. (see the movie "Dances with Wolves")

The desire for power is a result of catastrophes. Hunger, threat to life, or social degradation initiates a bodily panic, leading the person to try and control their environment to provide for future catastrophes.

This happened to Indo-European cattle drovers. Drought led to a shortage of plants, making cultivation of grain impossible. Every dry spell threatened the herd's survival. The ensuing panic caused the first patriarchs to create large herds to prevent shortage of food in times of need. Fear-driven behavior became a vicious cycle. The storing of cattle reserves created competitors and envy, and herds were stolen. One had to constantly increase one's power to keep control over cattle, supplies, land, and people. The vicious cycle has endured and continues to create existential dread, which in turn induces a striving for power (Adolf Adler identified this pattern back in 1912).

Power creates fear, not joy, for victims and the powerful alike. The rich are more threatened thieves, assassins, and kidnappers than the poor. They secure their wealth by hiring armies and building walls. Europe's fortresses and the palaces of the Maharajahs were first and foremost security systems to prevent assassinations. They were not very efficient, murder and homicide happened daily.

The hierarchy of power is a degeneration of species-appropriate human husbandry. It is useless, a sham posing as normalcy, as abnormal as caged circus animals.

Technological progress led to a level of prosperity which fulfills our basic needs of nourishment and security in developed countries. Material affluence is gained through extreme deficits in social devotion and self-actualization. Both have no economic value in a capitalist market design. It is no coincidence that the disregarded faculties of women lie in these two areas.

Anyone with a happy childhood will remember the love they received from their mother, unconditionally supporting their development. Most adults are lonely and unsure of their self-worth. Therein lies the decisive development potential of the future. What we need is a revaluation of the emotional abilities of mothers.

A new global currency

The future is here, even though experts do not realize how and why. The leading global currency, the US dollar, is currently being replaced by a new global currency, able to turn economic life inside out. None of the US president's defiant acts of violence will prevent it from happening.

So, who will replace the dollar; the renminbi, euro, rupee, or even bitcoin?

None of the above. The new leading currency has been in use globally for a long time. It is called Like.

Internet is very addictive for many people, all of them trying to get as many Likes, shares, emojis, and hearts as possible. Sounds idiotic, but that's how it is. Likes are a global currency for social acceptance and attention. Deficits make trade goods expensive. Care and attention are presently the scarcest commodity of civilization. Most people lack care and attention, respect, appreciation, praise, and love.

The internet provides all of that seemingly free of charge. Internet stars accumulate millions of followers who Like them, and spend their lives on maximizing their number of Likes.

One might smile at those people, but that's how it is. The love deficit pushes people to spend their money on the internet on some scam promising love.

Likes are not the most intelligent form of care but they unmask the mental state of users who play the puppet for Likes. We need to recognize and seriously examine our relationship needs in order to live a happy life in a progressing society.

Our emotional development mirrors that of grad school students, yearning for stars and stickers from their teacher. They are adequate as a means of approval, but the system needs to be improved. There is so much more that can lead us to bliss.

Love cannot be bought. It is gifted you, especially when you give it too.

Nothing is more precious than an honest smile.

Nothing encourages self-confidence more than honest appreciation.

Nothing fosters self-actualization better than honest devotion.

Nothing enriches life as much as respect and appreciation.

Devotion and appreciation cast out fear and make striving for power and prestige superfluous.

In this respect it is clear which direction the world of this century has to pursue. Insecure men need to know: low effort will lead to high reward. Appreciating women and heeding their call for devotion will be reciprocated with countless small gifts.

A smile from the cashier at the grocery store alone can make my day. Making her smile is not hard, so I keep receiving the nourishing warmth turning me into a child again, the child willing to do anything for its mother's smile.

A global movement to rescue Mother Earth

We only have one Earth. We should treat her better.

When "luminaries" like Stephen Hawking and Elon Musk see colonization of Mars as humanity's only way of salvation, seven billion people must cry out in dismay: "How ludicrous is that?!"

I am not against space travel as an expansion of our possibilities, but life and nature cannot be replaced that way.

Despite increasingly large telescopes, we have yet to find a planet as rich and full of life as our Earth. James Lovelock is right when he regards Gaia as its own living, self-regulating being. Gaia is the ancient Goddess and cares for us; always has. Even though we have been overstraining her patience for a long time, she is still well-disposed towards humankind.

It is time to come to our senses. If we continue the way we are now, we will eradicate all wonderful beings of the Goddess. She will set boundaries. Volcanoes can darken the sun in the blink of an eye, tsunamis will destroy cities, and earthquakes will level the stone witnesses of our hubris.

We will recognize the earth for what it is, our support.

This does not have to happen, and more and more people are actively fighting it. Men and women rise up against the madness of the powerful. The more people ally themselves with Mother Earth, the quicker we will save the world.

Paradise is a garden and Eden is in every planted garden. Earth is large enough for every individual (of soon to be 10 billion) to grow a small garden, or for a group to grow a large one. The ancient garden cultures of wise women were able to feed all people, healthy and without chemicals.

"[…] If you would be happy all your life, plant a garden" is the wisest Chinese proverb. Humankind is happy in a community and blissful among nature. The rules of nature are easy: Below there is steady rock, plants grow above and animals and humankind live next to each other. We can build stone cities if we grow gardens on their roofs. The future belongs to garden cities, urban and vertical farming. Anyone can prolong their life growing organic vegetables on the balcony.

Shamans of primitive people have been in the know all along. Everything is connected. Nature is spiritual, respecting her will keep the world in balance. Anyone communicating with nature knows they are surrounded by living beings. Christine Kessler (2016) and Carl von Siemens (2018) point out the enormous potential of knowledge of nature if integrated into our daily lives.

Children and adults are happy around animals. A dog, rabbit, squirrel, birds at a feeder – every encounter with beings is a moment of happiness. Is it not more beautiful to encounter and admire a deer in the forest than to kill it? I admire donkeys and their patient gaze, pigs and their jolly grunts, falcons, foxes, even the hundreds of spiders populating my garden. I no longer hate mosquitoes since I've learned how they strengthen my immune system. Flies are no longer irritating, they clean and caress my skin. The one thing I despise nowadays is people who torture animals, their suffering poisoning our souls.

All life is beautiful. Fish, frogs, snakes, lizards, the more the better.

The better one tends to their garden, the more animals will come to live in it.

Gardeners responsible for plants and animal are happy. They may shape nature as long as is serves life and its diversity. Life will then provide us with everything we need to live.

Mother Earth will smile. And we will feel her benevolence.

Acknowledgments

I have to thank Kirsten Armbruster and Rosemarie Hofstaetter who showed me the way to patriarchy criticism research, opening my eyes to the true causes of war.

Thanks to Marija Gimbutas and Gerhard Bott whose revolutionary discovery of matrivivial culture will change the world.

Many thanks to all mothers of this world who, after having suffered and tolerated so much over the millenia, still continue to bring us into this world and give us their love.

I thank all women and men who started down the path of returning to the origins of humanity, and helping to build a peaceful and healthy world.

May the Goddess be with us!

Bibliography

Adler, A: Über den nervösen Charakter. Vandenhoeck & Ruprecht 2008

Althoff, G. e.a.: Krieg im Mittelalter. Theiss 2017

Arlamovsky, M: Future Baby. Falter 2017

Armbruster, K: Das Muttertabu oder der Beginn von Religion. Editioncourage 2010

Armbruster, K: Gott, die MUTTER: Eine Streitschrift wider den patriarchalen Monotheismus. BoD 2013

Armbruster, K: Der Muschelwcg - Auf den Spuren von Gott, der Mutter: Die Wiederentdeckung der matrifokalen Wurzeln Europas. BoD 2014

Bode, Th: Die Diktatur der Konzerne. Fischer 2018

Bornemann, E: Das Patriarchat. Fischer 1974

Bornemann, E: Recht und Sexualität im griechischen Mythos. In: Lessing: Griechische Sagen. Bertelsmann 1984

Bott, G: Die Erfindung der Götter 2. BoD 2014

Böttcher, C.H: Der Ursprung Europas. Röhrig Universitätsverlag 2000.

Brand, U. und Wissen, M: Imperiale Lebensweise: Zur Ausbeutung von Mensch und Natur in Zeiten des globalen Kapitalismus. Ökom Vlg 2017

Bregman, R: Utopien für Realisten. Rowohlt 2017

Chotjewiez, P: Der Fall Hypatia. EVA 2002

Deschner, K: Kriminalgeschichte des Christentums. Bd 1-10. Rowohlt 1989

Dux, G: Die Spur der Macht im Verhältnis der Geschlechter. Springer 2019.

Fauvelle, F: Das goldene Rhinozeros. C.H.Beck 2017.

Felber, Ch: Die Gemeinwohl-Ökonomie. Deuticke 2010.

Ferretti, V: Radiographie der kollektiven Gewalttätigkeit. Feretti Vlg 2017

Flasch, K: Warum ich kein Christ bin. C.H.Beck 2015

Fleck, L: Entstehung und Entwicklung einer wissenschaftlichen Tatsache. Suhrkamp 1980.

Fried, J: Kein Tod auf Golgatha. C.H.Beck 2019

Gasperl, H: Die geheime Kraft aus der Erde. Servus 2018

Gielen, M: Zu Nazareth geboren? In: Salzburger Nachrichten 19.1.19, Wochenendbeilage S 11

Gimbutas, M: Göttinnen und Götter im Alten Europa. Arun Vlg 2010

Goltermann, S: Opfer – Die Wahrnehmung von Krieg und Gewalt in der Moderne. Fischer 2016

Harari, Y: Eine kurze Geschichte der Menschheit. Pantheon 2015

Harari, Y: 21 Lektionen für das 21. Jhdt. C.H.Beck 2018

Haarmann, H: Lexikon der untergegangenen Sprachen. C.H.Beck 2002

Haarmann, H: Einführung in die Donauschrift. Buske 2010.

Haarmann, H: Geschichte der Sintflut. C.H.Beck 2013

Haarmann, H: Wer zivilisierte die alten Griechen? Marix Vlg 2017

Horx, M: Das Megatrend-Prinzip. Pantheon 2014

Kessler, C: Wilder Geist, Wildes Herz. Kamphausen 2016

Klarsicht-Blog: Der Mithras-Kult und das Christentum. Klarsicht 2013/12. https://religionskritik4.blogspot.com/2013/12/der-mithraskult-und-das-christentum-die.html?m=1&fbclid=IwAR2e2GhwK5xGwv-4xkC-3X_xNQSFk4CFIzCZiFLClHOGsi3HCJBy8tzTnVU

Leppin, H: Die frühen Christen. C.H.Beck 2018

Liedloff, J: Auf der Suche nach dem verlorenen Glück. C.H.Beck 2017

Lüders, M: Wer den Wind sät. C.H.Beck 2018

Lorenz, K: Das sogenannte Böse. Dtv 1998

Lovelock, J: Gaia, die Erde ist ein Lebewesen. Fischer 1992

Mann, C. e.a.: Amerika vor Kolumbus: Die Geschichte eines unentdeckten Kontinents. Rowohlt 2016

Maslow, A: Die Psychologie des Seins. Kindler 1973

Meulemann, H: Ohne Kirche leben. Springer 2018

Moosbauer G: Die vergessene Römerschlacht. C.H.Beck 2018

Morland, P: Die Macht der Demographie. Ecowin 2019

Müller, K: Familiengeheimnisse. In: Die Wienerin 2014/4. https://wienerin.at/mit-familienaufstellung-probleme-losen

Naimark, N: Genozid. Theiss 2018

Opelt, R: Die Kinder des Tantalus. Czernin 2002.

Opelt, R: Familienmuster. Czernin 2008.

Opelt, R: Amors vergiftete Pfeile. Kneipp Vlg Wien 2009

Opelt, R: Tantalus´Welt. amazon/kdp 2016

Opelt, R: Die Königin von Kreta: Stiersspringer. amazon/kdp 2017

Opelt, R: 2100. Die neue Welt. amazon/kdp 2018

Orwell, G: 1984. Ullstein 1994

Pahl, H: Genese, Konsolidierung und Transformation der neoklassischen Wissenschaftskultur: Zur Konturierung einer Soziologie der Wirtschaftswissenschaften. Springer 2017

Parzinger, H: Die Kinder des Prometheus. C.H.Beck 2016

Pinker, S: Aufklärung jetzt. Fischer 2018

Reinhard, W: Die Unterwerfung der Welt. C.H.Beck 2018

Ringel, E. e.a.: Religionsverlust durch religiöse Erziehung. Herder 1993
Rinke, S: Conquistadoren und Azteken. C.H.Beck 2019
Rogers, C: Entwicklung der Persönlichkeit. Klett-Cotta 2018
Rublack, U: Der Astronom und die Hexe. Klett-Cotta 2018
Schmöckel, R: Die Morgenröte der alten Welt. BoD 2015
Schulmeister, S: Der Weg zur Prosperität. Ecowin 2018
Seitz, V: Afrika wird armregiert. Dtv 2018
Seville, A: Der Sound der Macht. C.H.Beck 2018
Toynbee, A: Der Gang der Weltgeschichte. 4 Bände. Dtv 1970
Uhlmann, G: Archäologie und Macht. BoD 2012
Uhlmann, G: Der Gott im 9. Monat. BoD 2015
Von Siemens, C: Der Tempel der magischen Tiere. Malik 2018
Von Werlhof, C: Die Verkehrung. Promedia 2011
Weixlbaumer, E: Wer´s glaubt. Goldegg 2017
Wolf, D: Das wunderbare Vermächtnis der Steinzeit. BoD 2017
Wunn, I: Götter-Gene-Genesis. Springer 2014
Wunn, I: Barbaren, Geister, Gotteskrieger. Springer 2017

Readers' comments

Kirsten Armbruster: This is a great, eye-opening text. My husband and I visited Spreewald, the Lausitz, Görlitz and the Czech Republic this summer, meeting the Sorbs for the first time. The trips took on a new level of meaning. Thanks.

Rosemarie Hofstaetter: If religions never existed, our worldly structures of life would look very different. We would life close to the ground in unison with nature instead of steep pyramidal structures. Feelings of guilt and inferiority complexes would barely exist. Sex and relationships would be natural, having children would be unproblematic. Equality of man and woman would be self-evident and the freedom of self-actualization the biggest gift. There would be less abnormality, prostitution, or perversity; the inner spirit being FREE instead of trapped. We would be able to love ourselves and recognize the love in others. Wars would be rare and hunger would not exist.

Jötunn Kadi: This outstanding summary could be expanded by including the chain of proselytizations and colonization spread to new continents by emotionally burdened Germans.

Sonja Raab: Wow. I've rarely read such a summary on the topic! Thank you for the effort and for publishing it! Very fascinating. There is much yet to do.

Beate Hofmann: You are rewriting history for me, just like Kirsten Armbruster. I am not an expert in the field, but was experiencing, even as a child, diffuse shame and a great inexplicable unease about our history. This clarifies many a thing...

Read on?

Below more books by S.A.W. publishing

First two books are translated to English, others in German with English short text.

Tantalus' world:

Why do wars exist? Is violence part of a human's being? Can mental pain be traced back to war and violence?

Experiencing extreme violence shapes national consciousness. Victory and defeat; a nation's most significant warlike incidents of the past can explain its character – optimistic or pessimistic, defensive or offensive. War is an effective means of obtaining power. The most brutal warriors are branded heroes in national histories.

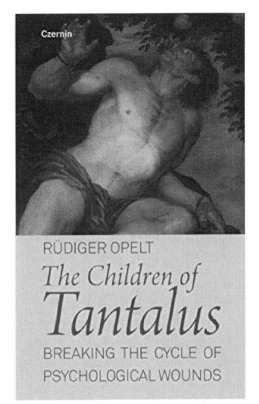

We slowly begin to understand that we cannot afford wars on our cramped planet anymore. Still, grenades and rifles are resonating in peoples' souls. Bellicose men deny the damages and are thus anchoring violence in our spirits. This is a vicious cycle repeating for generations. National catastrophes, like World War I, the Russian revolution, or the Chinese civil war, traumatize entire nations and damage their structures. The developing national traumas can only be processed during long periods of peace.

To prevent the world from falling to war and destruction, we have to overcome national traumas and replace the cycle of violence with productive global structures. Such solutions are presented in this book. The choice of a world worth living in is in our hands.

Without pain:

A young man wakes up next to a dead woman who is covered with blood. The victim is lying on his bed and the murder weapon is in his hand. He immediately becomes the primary suspect in the woman's slaying, although he insists that he knows neither the woman nor how she came to be in his bed. The path to solving the mystery follows a winding course through time and space. Important scenes occur in Austria in 1991, Prague in 1968, the Nazi concentration camp at Terezin during World War II, and a psychiatric ward in Moscow in 1991. The major characters range from the police inspector and his suspect to ruthless villains, helpless victims, a shyster lawyer, and a KGB hit man, all of whom are involved in a complex story line dealing with terrible family secrets, diabolical genetic research projects, a love affair that has gone sour, and crimes with international repercussions. The result is a powerful portrait of the psychology of violence.

Das Glück der Kinder:

Who doesn't want to live in a happy family? Many people view family as the most important thing in life. Family is expected to be shaped by loving contact with one another. It is supposed to provide shelter, security, and safety for growing children. This is not a given. Cooperation has to be cultivated, and conflicts have to be resolved. The upbringing on kids needs time, strong nerves, and patience. In order to fulfill those requirements one has to know what to look for and how to facilitate happy relationships among families.

Im Schatten des Kriegers:

Günter Kahowez grew up thinking that his father died a hero in Russia. The only thing Günter had left of him was his violin. Günter follows his father's ideal, becoming a composer and professor at the Conservatory of Music in Vienna.

At age 52 Günter discovers his father's lost journal of the campaign in Poland and Russia. All of a sudden he sees the pictures his father took there with entirely new eyes. Nothing will be the same.

Die Macht der schwarzen Magier:

The 20th century left a trail of destruction around the entire globe, sacrificing hundreds of millions people, thousands of animal species, and dozens of ecosystems. How did it come to this? Some victims of the collective terror must have thought their cruel fate a sign of an evil force. Supposing medieval man was right in his belief in demonic powers, 20th century history could have played out in the way this book describes.

Dalmatien- wie ich Anker warf und ein Haus sanierte: Eine Liebeserklärung in mehreren Ebenen.

Boating in the eastern Adriatic Sea; buying and renovating a house on a central Croatian island (Dugi Otok). Entertaining narrative including many pictures. A homage to the Croatian island world, explored by ship and through renovating a house. The story of the Croatians (Illyrians) retold.

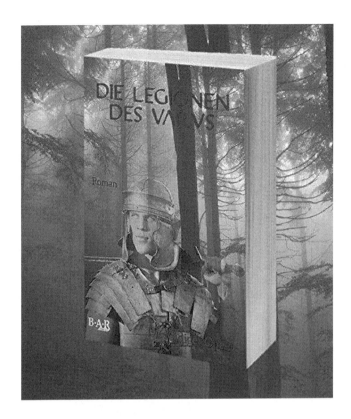

Die Legionen des Varus:

The Roman empire were victorious in countless battles. At the height of its glory it suffered a fiasco which helped found the myth of the German nation. The legions of Varus decided the fate of Europe.
This book is structured in two parts:

Part 1 is a piece of fiction describing the victory of Varus, which could have shaped the fate of Europe in an entirely different way.

Part 2 describes the factual succession of events following Varus' defeat.

Protest der Jungen:
(youth rebellion):

The old generation leaves a mess to the young, whose future seems lost. House prizes exploud, so do deficits and destruction of nature. Greta Thunberg und the member of Fridays for future press for change. When they will be in power, climate and diversity may collapse and social security as well. They have started do deal with the future so not to lose all chances.

Vier Wochen für Franz Ferdinand

In 1917 Germany was in the process of winning World War I. The USA wanted to prevent this from happening under any circumstances, joining the war after its fate had already been decided. America then ascended to become the biggest superpower of the world. The conceivable German victory would have led to a continental European customs union under German leadership by 1918. The same thing we now have under Angela Merkel. The madness of the intermediate 100 years was unnecessary and led humanity and the planet to the brink of demise. Germany would have unified Europe in 1918, and Hitler and Stalin would have never risen to power. 100 lost years making us tremble for the future of our Earth. Contrary to their propaganda the USA did not bring democracy to the world but capitalism, oligarchy, and environmental destruction. A throwaway society and the oil industry produced the greenhouse effect and destabilized the Middle East. None of this would have happened under the technologically leading Germans 100 years ago. German scientists were too productive for oil and nuclear industries to obtain the comprehensive, environmentally destructive relevance it has today. If only Germany was left to develop and advance in peace.

This book shows how a trivial things could have changed the course of the 20th century. If Austrian heir to the throne Franz Ferdinand had been shot four weeks later, he would have fired his incapable head of General Staff, which in turn would have stabilized the Russian front. The war would have ended in 1917 and the 20th century would have taken a more peaceful and environmentally friendly course.

Be surprised with possible historic turnarounds had the victors England and the USA not botched the 20th century to the point of leading the planet to the brink of the abyss.

Das Ende des Patriarchats:
(The end of patriarchy):

Mighty men are destroying natur, burning jungles, killing indigenious peoples, the climate, the fish und the sea. Men have been trying to fight against these cruelties, but the military have showed them again and again who is in power. Patriarchy and scientist payed by the powerful have reduced our world to money and force.

Till we wake up from our brain-washed state of mind, we should listen to women. They love children and life and care for all living creatrues. That is why they have been slaughtered, oppressed and ignored in the past. By the wisdom of women we may return to a world of nature, love, beauty und peace.

Ganzheitsdenken:
(Holistic thinking –
wisdom oft the old ones)

Ever since the old ones habe been modells und keeper of traditions. They see connections unknown to the young ones. Soon old folks will be the majority in many countries and this makes sense: We need more holistic thinking to cope with a more and more complex world. Details and studies are not enough, we need an overview, that wise men used to have in all eras.

To save the world we need a fusion of science and holistic thinking

Dr. Rüdiger Opelt, born 1953 in Linz,

Psychologist, psychotherapist, seminar instructor, lecturer, author.

Rüdiger explored the causes of psychosomatic sickness and suffering in humans for 40 years. He found the origin of our psychological problems in the errors of the past, in war, violence, pain, and loneliness. He has published his thesis in multiple books (Die Kinder des Tantalus, Familienmuster, Tantalus' Welt).

For ten years he has combed through social science and natural science literature to discover the errors of our global society. He is convinced of the need to complement expert innovations with laterally thinking generalists in order to course correct humankind. Multiple of his books verify that the past could have played out very differently had there been a generalist science (Die Legionen des Varus, Vier Wochen für Franz Ferdinand, Die Macht der schwarzen Magier).

This book details his positive concept for the 21st century.

www.opelt.com   r@opelt.com

Rüdiger Opelt lives in Salzburg, has been married for 36 years and raised two children.

Rüdiger Opelt has published 24 books, of which three have been translated into English.

Made in the USA
Lexington, KY
04 November 2019